WORLD
HISTORY SERIES

Ancient Chinese Dynasties

Titles in the World History Series

The Age of Augustus
The Age of Exploration
The Age of Feudalism
The Age of Napoleon
The Age of Pericles
The Alamo
America in the 1960s
The American Frontier
The American Revolution
Ancient Chinese Dynasties
Ancient Greece
The Ancient Near East
Architecture
Aztec Civilization
The Battle of the
   Little Bighorn
The Black Death
The Byzantine Empire
Caesar's Conquest of Gaul
The California Gold Rush
The Chinese Cultural
   Revolution
The Civil Rights Movement
The Collapse of the
   Roman Republic
Colonial America
The Conquest of Mexico
The Constitution and the Founding
   of America
The Crimean War
The Crusades
The Cuban Missile Crisis
The Cuban Revolution
The Early Middle Ages
Egypt of the Pharaohs
Elizabethan England
The End of the Cold War
The Enlightenment
The French and Indian War
The French Revolution
The Glorious Revolution
The Great Depression
Greek and Roman
   Mythology
Greek and Roman Science
Greek and Roman Sport
Greek and Roman Theater
The History of Rock & Roll

The History of Slavery
Hitler's Reich
The Hundred Years' War
The Incan Empire
The Industrial Revolution
The Inquisition
The Italian Renaissance
The Late Middle Ages
The Lewis and Clark
   Expedition
The Making of the Atom Bomb
The Mexican-American War
The Mexican Revolution
The Mexican War of
   Independence
Modern Japan
The Mongol Empire
The Persian Empire
Prohibition
The Punic Wars
The Reagan Years
The Reformation
The Relocation of the North
   American Indian
The Renaissance
The Rise and Fall of the
   Soviet Union
The Roaring Twenties
The Roman Empire
The Roman Republic
Roosevelt and the
   New Deal
The Russian Revolution
Russia of the Tsars
The Salem Witch Trials
The Scientific Revolution
The Spread of Islam
The Stone Age
The Titanic
Traditional Africa
Traditional Japan
The Travels of Marco Polo
Twentieth Century Science
The War of 1812
The Wars of the Roses
The Watts Riot
Women's Suffrage

WORLD HISTORY SERIES

Ancient Chinese Dynasties

by
Eleanor J. Hall

Lucent Books, P.O. Box 289011, San Diego, CA 92198-9011

Library of Congress Cataloging-in-Publication Data

Hall, Eleanor J.
    Ancient Chinese dynasties / Eleanor J. Hall.
       p.   cm.—(World history series)
    Includes bibliographical references and index.
    Summary: Discusses the history, culture, material
artifacts, and society of six ancient Chinese dynasties from
about 2000 B.C. to 221 A.D.
    ISBN 1-56006-624-5 (alk. paper)
    1. China—History—To 221 B.C. Juvenile literature.
2. China—History—Ch'in dynasty, 221–207 B.C. Juvenile
literature. 3. China—History—Han dynasty, 202 B.C.–220 A.D.
Juvenile literature. [1. China—History—To 221 B.C.
2. China—History—Ch'in dynasty, 221–207 B.C. 3. China—
History—Han dynasty, 202 B.C.–220 A.D.] I. Title. II. Series.
DS741.5.H295 2000
931—dc21   99-37242
                                            CIP

Copyright 2000 by Lucent Books, Inc., P.O. Box 289011,
San Diego, California 92198-9011

Printed in the U.S.A.

Contents

Foreword

Each year on the first day of school, nearly every history teacher faces the task of explaining why his or her students should study history. One logical answer to this question is that exploring what happened in our past explains how the things we often take for granted—our customs, ideas, and institutions—came to be. As statesman and historian Winston Churchill put it, "Every nation or group of nations has its own tale to tell. Knowledge of the trials and struggles is necessary to all who would comprehend the problems, perils, challenges, and opportunities which confront us today." Thus, a study of history puts modern ideas and institutions in perspective. For example, though the founders of the United States were talented and creative thinkers, they clearly did not invent the concept of democracy. Instead, they adapted some democratic ideas that had originated in ancient Greece and with which the Romans, the British, and others had experimented. An exploration of these cultures, then, reveals their very real connection to us through institutions that continue to shape our daily lives.

Another reason often given for studying history is the idea that lessons exist in the past from which contemporary societies can benefit and learn. This idea, although controversial, has always been an intriguing one for historians. Those who agree that society can benefit from the past often quote philosopher George Santayana's famous statement, "Those who cannot remember the past are condemned to repeat it." Historians who subscribe to Santayana's philosophy believe that, for example, studying the events that led up to the major world wars or other significant historical events would allow society to chart a different and more favorable course in the future.

Just as difficult as convincing students to realize the importance of studying history is the search for useful and interesting supplementary materials that present historical events in a context that can be easily understood. The volumes in Lucent Books' World History Series attempt to present a broad, balanced, and penetrating view of the march of history. Ancient Egypt's important wars and rulers, for example, are presented against the rich and colorful backdrop of Egyptian religious, social, and cultural developments. The series engages the reader by enhancing historical events with these cultural contexts. For example, in *Ancient Greece*, the text covers the role of women in that society. Slavery is discussed in *The Roman Empire*, as well as how slaves earned their freedom. The numerous and varied aspects of every-day life in these and other societies are explored in each volume of the series. Additionally, the series covers the major political, cultural, and philosophical ideas as the torch of civilization is passed from ancient Mesopotamia and Egypt, through Greece, Rome, Medieval Europe, and other world cultures, to the modern day.

The material in the series is formatted in a thorough, precise, and organized manner. Each volume offers the reader a comprehensive and clearly written overview of an important historical event or period. The topic under discussion is placed in a broad, historical context. For example, *The Italian Renaissance* begins with a discussion of the High Middle Ages and the loss of central control that allowed certain Italian cities to develop artistically. The book ends by looking forward to the Reformation and interpreting the societal changes that grew out of the Renaissance. Thus, students are not only involved in an historical era, but also enveloped by the events leading up to that era and the events following it.

One important and unique feature in the World History Series is the primary and secondary source quotations that richly supplement each volume. These quotes are useful in a number of ways. First, they allow students access to sources they would not normally be exposed to because of the difficulty and obscurity of the original source. The quotations range from interesting anecdotes to farsighted cultural perspectives and are drawn from historical witnesses both past and present. Second, the quotes demonstrate how and where historians themselves derive their information on the past as they strive to reach a consensus on historical events. Lastly, all of the quotes are footnoted, familiarizing students with the citation process and allowing them to verify quotes and/or look up the original source if the quote piques their interest.

Finally, the books in the World History Series provide a detailed launching point for further research. Each book contains a bibliography specifically geared toward student research. A second, annotated bibliography introduces students to all the sources the author consulted when compiling the book. A chronology of important dates gives students an overview, at a glance, of the topic covered. Where applicable, a glossary of terms is included.

In short, the series is designed not only to acquaint readers with the basics of history, but also to make them aware that their lives are a part of an ongoing human saga. Perhaps they will then come to the same realization as famed historian Arnold Toynbee. In his monumental work, *A Study of History*, he wrote about becoming aware of history flowing through him in a mighty current, and of his own life "welling like a wave in the flow of this vast tide."

IMPORTANT DATES IN THE HISTORY
OF ANCIENT CHINESE DYNASTIES

2000 B.C.
The first Chinese dynasty, the Xia, is founded by Yu the Great. No archaeological evidence for this dynasty has yet been discovered but traditional Chinese literary sources tell of its existence.

202
Liu Bang subdues his rivals and is proclaimed emperor of a new dynasty called the Han. He chooses the name Gao Zu as his official title.

771
Discontented clan leaders of the Zhou dynasty stage a rebellion and reduce the Zhou emperors to mere figureheads.

210
Shi Huangdi dies and the Qin dynasty begins to lose control of the empire.

1050
The Shang are overthrown by one of their vassal states, the Zhou. The early leaders of the Zhou dynasty rule wisely and encourage learning. A Chinese literary classic, the *I Ching*, or *Book of Change* is published.

247
King Zheng of the state of Qin ascends the throne of his state and begins a long campaign of conquest to unite all the warring states under his leadership.

2000 B.C.	1500	1000	500 400 300

1600
The Xia dynasty is overthrown by the Shang clan whose rulers establish a powerful new dynasty. Bronze weapons are introduced and Shang artisans create magnificent bronze artworks. Writing is also developed.

551
Chinese teacher and philosopher, Confucius, is born. Other important philosophies, such as Daoism, also come to prominence as social thinkers try to reform governments and improve the lives of the common people.

403
Warring States period begins. Powerful states within the Zhou dynasty fight each other for control. Iron weapons and the crossbow appear.

221
King Zheng achieves final victory. He becomes emperor of a united China and takes the name Shi Huangdi or First Emperor. He abolishes the feudal system and sets up a strong, centralized government over which he rules absolutely.

207
Peasant warrior Liu Bang marches against the Qin capital and accepts the surrender of the emperor. A fight among rebel bands for control of the empire ensues.

188
Emperor Gao Zu dies, having established a strong and prosperous dynasty.

141
Gao Zu's great-great-grandson, Wu Di, ascends the throne and begins a long reign during which the Han dynasty prospers and expands through diplomacy and war.

100
One of ancient China's most distinguished historians, Sima Qian, publishes the first history of China called *Records of the Historian.*

87
Emperor Wu Di dies. Succeeding emperors are unable to deal effectively with the growing economic and social problems confronting the vast Chinese empire.

618
The Sui dynasty is overthrown by the Tang dynasty, ending China's period of ancient history. For the next three hundred years the Tang dynasty leads China to new heights of political power and outstanding cultural accomplishments.

A.D. 9
Wang Mang, a high official in the Han court, usurps the throne.

200	100	0	A.D. 100	200	300	400	500	600

23
Wang Mang is overthrown by a rebellion of peasants and land owners. A struggle ensues among descendants of previous Han emperors for control of the empire.

25
Guang Wu Di triumphs over other contenders for the throne and restores the Han dynasty.

220
The last Han emperor, Xien Di, resigns. The empire splits into three separate kingdoms and later splinters into many more.

184
A massive rebellion by the Yellow Turbans, a religious group seeking better conditions for the poor, weakens the Han dynasty.

581
China is reunited under the Sui dynasty which lasts only thirty-seven years.

189
Two thousand eunuchs (court officials in charge of the women's quarters) are massacred by imperial military forces because they have become too powerful in the imperial court.

The First Dynasties

In ancient China, leadership was decided by force. Powerful clans vied for control of vast territories. Defeated clans became vassal states whose role was to support the victorious clan by paying tribute and by supplying workers and soldiers to serve their conquerors. Vassal states that caused trouble or showed signs of rebelliousness were dealt with swiftly and harshly.

Victorious clans often founded dynasties, a term referring to a succession of rulers from the same family or clan. Although the ruling dynasty was the supreme authority, vassal states were often allowed to keep their own identities as long as they remained subservient. The result was a collection of semi-independent states dominated by a powerful dynasty.

Some dynasties ruled only a part of what is today known as China, while others ruled over most of the country, unifying what had previously been a collection of individual fiefdoms. Some dynasties endured for hundreds of years, while others lasted only a brief time.

THE FOUNDING OF DYNASTIES

According to early Chinese histories, the first dynasty in China was the Xia, which was founded about 2000 B.C. As yet, no firm archaeological evidence for the Xia has been discovered, but strong literary traditions argue for its existence.

The first dynasty in ancient China whose presence has been proven unquestionably is the Shang, which came to power about 1600 B.C. (Dates for the early dynasties vary from scholar to scholar

Scholars are absolutely certain of the existence of the Shang dynasty, whose history is documented with relics like this bronze cooking vessel from Ningxian, China.

and will doubtless undergo further revision in light of continuing archaeological research.)

Like the Xia, the Shang dynasty was once considered mythical. Excavations in the early twentieth century, however, proved its existence. Archaeologists were astonished to find an abundance of skillfully made bronze objects in Shang ruins, including weapons, tools, urns, wine vessels, and bells. Excavators also found inscriptions on animal bones and tortoise shells used by Shang kings and their advisers to foretell the future. Because scholars were able to translate the inscriptions, a great deal is known today about life in the Shang dynasty.

Around 1050 B.C., the Shang dynasty was overthrown by the Zhou, one of its vassal states. After subduing the Shang, leaders of the Zhou established the longest dynasty in Chinese history, one that lasted about eight hundred years. Though strong and powerful for the first half of their rule, Zhou kings later became mere figureheads as rival groups challenged their supremacy. About 221 B.C. another powerful clan, the Qin, overthrew the Zhou. The Qin conquered all the other warring factions as well and created the first unified Chinese empire. Their powerful leader, King Zheng, later took the title of Qin Shi Huangdi—First Emperor of China.

A number of political and social improvements were instituted under the Qin dynasty. One major undertaking was the building of a network of roads to facilitate travel and bind the vast empire together. Since it was the common people who sup-

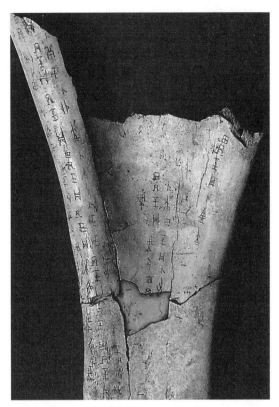

Much of what is known about the Shang dynasty comes from inscriptions on oracle bones, which were used to predict future events.

plied the labor and taxes to build roads and other projects (such as royal palaces and defensive walls), rebellions began to break out even before the first emperor died.

A few years after the emperor's death, the Qin dynasty was toppled by Liu Bang, a peasant warrior, who established the Han dynasty in 206 B.C. Through the centuries that followed, Han emperors greatly expanded China's territorial boundaries by means of both diplomacy and conquest. The Han dynasty reached the height of its power around the first century A.D.

Like other dynasties before it, the powerful Han dynasty eventually weakened and fell due to corruption in government, extravagance within the imperial court, natural disasters, and rival clans. The next four centuries were ones of civil strife as state after state fought to control all the others. Not until the sixth century A.D. did China again become united.

SOCIAL AND CULTURAL ACHIEVEMENTS

In spite of the ongoing wars and political turbulence that characterized ancient China, this time was also one of great so-cial and cultural achievement. Even in the worst of times, scholars, philosophers, poets, artists, architects, inventors, and technicians created lasting works that continue to amaze the world thousands of years later.

Of these achievements, one immensely important innovation was the development of writing, which first appeared around 1600 B.C., during the Shang dynasty. Except for some changes introduced during the Qin dynasty (to standardize the script), Chinese writing remained relatively constant throughout the ages. Chinese writing and speaking are not connected as they are in languages based on alphabetic systems. While there

AN ALPHABET FOR THE CHINESE LANGUAGE?

With a few modifications, Chinese writing has remained amazingly constant since its ancient origins. In recent years, however, a movement has arisen to create an alphabet in place of the thousands of characters Chinese readers have to learn. In the following excerpt taken from Cultural Atlas of China, *authors Caroline Blunden and Mark Elvin describe this effort and its chances of success.*

Early in the twentieth century a movement started to create a "national language" based on "official speech." The aim was that this should be spoken by everyone, if only as a second language. First under the Nationalists, and now under the present government, this rather artificial language has become widespread. The basic motivation for this unification of the spoken language was and remains political. But there is a further potential advantage: once everyone's pronunciation is much the same, it will be possible to replace the old characters with an al-phabetic system, without impairing national inter-communication. The time when this will be possible is sometime off. If ever decided upon, it would con-stitute a dramatic cultural rupture with the past.

The Pinyin System of Pronunciation

Translating Chinese into English has presented enormous challenges to scholars. Several translation schemes were devised in the late nineteenth and early twentieth centuries; until recently, the Wade-Giles system was most widely used. In 1979 the Chinese government adopted the pinyin system, based on the Mandarin dialect. Pronunciations for selected vowels and consonants used in pinyin are excerpted here, as they appear in The Great Bronze Age of China, *edited by Wen Fong.*

Notes on Romanization and Pronunciation

Vowels

a	as in **fa**ther, but not as in **ta**nk
ang	as in **ang**le (Shang dynasty)
ai	as in wh**y** (Shanghai city)
ao	as in **ou**t (Chairman Mao)
ei	as in **ei**ght (Wei dynasty, Beijing)
eng	as in yo**ung** (Zhengzhou city)
i	generally as in mach**i**ne (Jilin, Xi River) although the pronunciation varies depending upon the consonant preceding it
ia	as in Malays**ia** (Xia dynasty)
iu	pronounced **yo** (Liu, a surname)
ou	as in s**ou**l (Zhou dynasty)
ua	as in w**a**ffle (Hua, a surname)
uai	pronounced **why** (Huai River)

Consonants

c	as in ha**ts** or pa**ts**y
q	as in **ch**air (Qin dynasty)
x	as in **sh**ip (Xian city)
y	as in **y**ellow (Yangtze River)
zh	as in **J**oe (Zhou dynasty)

were (and still are) many dialects of Chinese speech, there is only one written language.

Historian Derk Bodde emphasizes the importance of this fact: "Of all the cultural forces that have made for political as well as cultural unity [in China], there is little question that the uniformity of the written language (in contrast to the diversity of the spoken dialects) has been more influential than any other."[1]

Legacy of the Ancient Chinese Dynasties

Writing is just one of many cultural innovations surviving from China's past.

Many contemporary social customs, styles of art, religious beliefs, and philosophies are also firmly rooted in ancient Chinese history. While all modern societies display traces of their history to one degree or another, Christopher Hibbert, author of *The Emperors of China*, believes the steadfast transmission of cultural traits through the ages accounts for the endurance of aspects of Chinese civilization long after other ancient societies have perished:

> This continuity, indeed, is the most striking aspect of Chinese civilization.

It is not old when compared with the civilizations of India and the Middle East: King Cheops' pyramid at Giza was built more than eight hundred years before the Hsia [Xia] Dynasty is said to have been founded; Troy flourished; and the palace of Knossos rose on Crete long before the Shang civilization appeared. But the earlier civilizations did not endure; the Chinese did.[2]

Understanding something of ancient China and its dynasties helps to understand modern China as well.

Chapter

1 The Xia Dynasty: Mythical or Real?

In early Chinese literature, one of the most esteemed heroes is Huangdi, the Yellow Emperor, a name probably derived from the color of the Chinese soil. "His list of achievements is endless," write historians Edmund Capon and William MacQuitty. "He is recorded as having invented wheeled vehicles, armour, ships and pottery, as well as drawing up regulations concerning religious ceremonies and sacrifices."[3]

The Yellow Emperor is one of many superhuman leaders depicted in Chinese folklore who supposedly carried out prodigious tasks such as creating fire and inventing writing. Whether these distant figures were entirely fictional or real persons whose attributes were simply overblown has been debated in scholarly circles for centuries.

Even Sima Qian, China's first historian, faced this problem in the first century B.C. when he began writing a history of China, called *Records of the Historian*. After an intensive study of documents and other evidence about the past that was available to him, Sima Qian chose to include stories of the Yellow Emperor in his history. In *Records of the Historian*, he reports that the

Yellow Emperor had several wives and many sons, but at that time, there was no definite pattern of imperial succession. Consequently, for several generations after the Yellow Emperor's death, the throne passed back and forth among his descendants.

Around the middle of the twenty-third century B.C., a great-great-grandson of the Yellow Emperor, named Yao, ascended the throne at the age of sixteen. Like his illustrious ancestor, Yao gained the love and respect of his people by ruling benignly and wisely. Later in Yao's reign, however, floods devastated the land, causing havoc and threatening to break up the empire. In desperation, Yao searched for a capable person who could help him find ways to control the floods.

Yao had heard good reports about a man named Shun, whom he persuaded to serve as one of his aides. To test Shun, Yao repeatedly challenged him with difficult tasks, which Shun always completed successfully. Satisfied that Shun was the man to save the empire, Yao asked him to become co-emperor. Historian K. C. Wu explains:

There were to be two emperors at the same time, one reigning, one ruling. Yao was the reigning emperor, in whose name every order would be decreed and everything executed. But Shun would be the co-emperor to decree and to execute. In other words, except in name, Shun was to bear the responsibility of the empire alone. It was he and he only who would have to see that the flood was checked, the people given safety and prosperity, and the empire restored to its effectiveness and glory.[4]

THE REIGN OF EMPEROR SHUN

Once installed as emperor, Shun quickly tackled the problems of flood control,

---

LEGENDS OF YU THE GREAT

Although the existence of Yu the Great has never been proven, many stories about his admirable character were recorded by ancient Chinese historians. Using these sources, author K. C. Wu reviews the fine qualities of Yu the Great in his book The Chinese Heritage.

Whatever measure of greatness we may attribute to Yu, there is no question but that he was as selfless and as dedicated to the well-being of the people of the empire as either of his two predecessors [Kings Yao and Shun]. Nevertheless, he has left with us an impression distinctly different from both Yao and Shun. For, manifestly, he was made of much sterner stuff. . . . He was never sparing of himself, not only physically . . . but mentally and morally too. Every time he heard someone criticize him, he would make a low obeisance [bow] in deep appreciation. He detested idling. Often when he saw the change of a shade in the sun, even though it was but by an inch, he would express regret that he had not accomplished anything during that brief passage of time. He was as contemptuous as he was apprehensive of luxury and of pleasures. One bit of advice he used to give was later put into a song by his descendants:

> When the palace is a wild of lust,
> And the country is a wild for hunting;
> When wine is sweet, and music the delight;
> When there are lofty roofs and carved walls;—
> The existence of any one of these things
> Has never been but the prelude to ruin.

traveling to the worst disaster sites to see the effects firsthand. As a result, he became convinced that the methods used by Yao's chief engineer, a man named Gun, were inadequate. Gun's methods consisted mainly of building dikes, which had proved ineffective against the rising waters. When Gun refused to try new approaches, Shun dismissed him and appointed Yu, Gun's son, as the new engineer. Yu's approach to flood control consisted of channeling the rivers into the seas as quickly as possible instead of trying to hold them back. Yu tackled the job with such skill and determination that the floods were brought under control only a few years later.

THE FIRST DYNASTY

After Emperor Yao died, Shun elevated Yu to co-emperor, just as Yao had previously done for him. When Shun died, Yu prepared to turn the throne over to Shun's son, but Yu's grateful subjects prevailed upon him to continue as emperor.

Before becoming emperor, Yu had been made prince over a small kingdom called Xia. "So as emperor," Wu writes, ". . . the place name was appended to his name, and he was known as Xia Yu. And it is also from Xia that the Chinese, as a people, first acquired a name for themselves—the Xia people. Prior to this time, there is no record indicating that the Chinese had called themselves by any particular appellation."[5]

When it came time for Yu to pick a successor, ancient documents tell different stories. According to one account, Yu selected one of his ministers, named Yi, to be the next emperor, but Yu's son, Qi, rebelled and forcibly took over the throne. Another version agrees that Yu chose Yi, but reports that Qi became emperor because the people insisted on it, much as they had done for his father.

Regardless of which story is correct, Qi became emperor, and, Wu writes, "He did not hesitate to see to it that he himself was succeeded by his own son, thus establishing the first definitive dynasty in China—the Xia dynasty. And thenceforth hereditary succession became the rule."[6]

The new emperor did not possess the kindly characteristics of his predecessors. When his half-brother protested Qi's claim to the throne, Qi led his army against his kinsman and in the ensuing battle, the offending prince was killed and the people he had ruled were destroyed.

LATER XIA RULERS

The three emperors following Qi were men with little administrative ability who left the governing to others while they pursued lives of pleasure. Because the rulers neglected their responsibilities, the empire was gradually taken over by unscrupulous ministers who sought power for themselves. One such minister, Hanzhou, became so powerful during the reign of Emperor Xiang that he yielded to temptation and usurped the throne. In a surprise attack on the imperial palace, Hanzhou and his rebels killed Xiang and his entire family—or so they thought.

The Merging of Myth with History

Some of the early stories in the history of ancient China are obviously legendary, but as the tales move closer to historical times, the line between fact and fiction becomes harder to draw. Christopher Hibbert, in his book The Emperors of China, *addresses this problem in the following excerpt.*

China's ancient history merges into myth. In the beginning the world was an egg. When the egg cracked open, the top of the shell grew to become the sky, the lower part became the earth, and out of the middle stepped a man, P'an-ku, who lived for eighteen thousand years. Helped by a dragon, a phoenix, a unicorn, and a tortoise, P'an-ku worked hard, cutting the earth into shape, making the valleys and the mountains. And when he died his flesh became the earth's soil, his blood became the seas and rivers, his eyes the sun and moon, his breath the wind, his voice thunder. The parasites that fed upon his body became the ancestor of the human race. Such is the story told to Chinese children, over the generations.

In the earliest times the people that developed from P'an-ku's parasites were ruled by such supernaturally endowed hero-kings as Fu-shi, who taught men how to hunt and fish, to rear animals for food, and to write, who instructed them in philosophy and music and in living harmoniously with women in marriage. Other great rulers founded dynasties that lasted thousands of years and guided their people into an ever more civilized life.

These rulers gave the people institutions, which men in later times looked back upon as models of perfection. They encouraged piety and sacrifices to the gods, regard for the family and veneration for ancestors; these have remained among the basics of Chinese culture. . . . The mists of legend begin to clear with Yu the great who created a vast system of drainage canals to protect the country from the floods that had previously inundated it and who, in the twenty-first century B.C., founded the Hsia [Xia] dynasty. But of that dynasty virtually nothing else is known apart from a list of its emperors, and skeptical historians have doubted its very existence. Some once doubted, too, the stories told of the Shang dynasty, which had, so it was said, succeeded the Hsia in the sixteenth century B.C. Yet, in the case of the Shang, modern archeology has proved the skeptics wrong.

Xiang's empress, who was pregnant, managed to escape and fled to the protection of her own clan. Shortly afterward, she bore a son, Shaokang. From early childhood, Shaokang was brought up with the expectation that he would one day bring down Hanzhou and restore the Xia dynasty. He dedicated himself to that goal, and with the help of other princes sympathetic to his cause, he eventually accomplished his mission.

In the final showdown, Hanzhou was killed in battle. Then, according to an ancient document called the *Bamboo Annals*, "Shaokang betook himself to Yu's old imperial seat, Anyi, north of the Yellow River, and was acknowledged by all the princes of the empire as their lawful sovereign."[7] Shaokang and his son Zhu, who succeeded him, ruled well and restored a measure of tranquility to the empire similar to that enjoyed under the earlier rulers.

LIFE IN THE EARLY XIA DYNASTY

While the political maneuverings of Xia emperors were taking place, everyday life during the Xia dynasty underwent significant changes. By modern reckoning, the Xia dynasty began about 2000 B.C., placing its founding somewhere between the late Neolithic (New Stone) Age and the early Bronze Age. During this important historical age Chinese civilization evolved from a nomadic hunting society to an agricultural one. Also during this period metal tools and weapons began to replace those made of wood and stone.

Traditional stories report that the transition from hunting to farming was encouraged by early rulers. For example, Emperor Shun created a department of agriculture in his government. He also took measures to protect farmers against devastating raids by nomadic tribes, which at that time were a frequent occurrence.

Archaeological excavations of settlements from the time and place at which the Xia would have ruled show that life was hard in this era. Houses were circular or square and had floors that consisted of shallow pits dug into the ground. The walls were wattle and daub—upright poles set into the ground, interwoven with branches and plastered with mud. Roofs were thatched with reeds and grass. Weapons and tools were still made principally of stone and wood.

Not every Xia emperor was convinced of the need for agriculture. Later in the Xia dynasty, in fact, most emperors not only failed to encourage agriculture but actively discouraged it. For example, Emperor Taikang, Yu the Great's grandson, enjoyed hunting and the nomadic lifestyle so much, he abolished the department of agriculture. "Taikang felt there was no longer any necessity for maintaining the ministry," Wu reports. "Agriculture had already been developed enough; to expand it further would be to reduce the more land area needed by the nomads."[8] Moreover, later emperors did nothing to protect farming villages.

Nevertheless, Taikang and other emperors antagonistic to agriculture were running against the cultural tide. Although Xia chronicles report an occasional reversion to nomadism, agriculture had firmly taken hold. Population steadily increased as life became more settled, and many villages expanded into large towns and cities. An even more dramatic change was coming, however.

LIFE IN THE XIA BRONZE AGE

Bronze metallurgy transformed the society through the creation of more efficient tools and weapons. The production of bronze was strictly controlled by the ruling classes, so weapons and other articles made from it were available only to elite groups. Bronze weapons gave Xia rulers greater control over their own subjects, making the development of dynastic rule much easier.

It was not just the ruling classes who saw change with the coming of the Bronze Age. Social class distinctions intensified among large segments of the population

It was during the Xia dynasty that Chinese life changed from being nomadic to being primarily agricultural.

During the Xia dynasty, bronze was often fashioned into weapons or religious objects, thereby reinforcing the power of China's rulers.

who now lived in sizable cities protected by massive earthen walls. Elite classes lived in lavish style while the lower classes struggled to exist. With few if any rights, the common people were conscripted as laborers to build defenses, palaces, and tombs for the elite. Thousands more were drafted into military service.

Bronze weapons also greatly enhanced the military power of Xia rulers, both for defending the empire and for conquering new territory. Other developments contributed to this growth of power. The Xia reportedly had acquired chariots, which they used in warfare. With such inventions as these, the conduct of war gradually became more organized and more deadly.

Besides raw force, Xia rulers also controlled their subjects through religious rites aimed at appeasing ancestral spirits, a form of worship already old in Xia times. Elevating these rites to high drama and coupling them with fear of the supernatural, Xia emperors exerted a psychological hold over their people. Sacred bronze ritual objects used in ancestor worship became powerful icons. Archaeologist Kwang-chih Chang believes this

dual use of bronze, for weapons and religious objects, underlay dynastic power in ancient China:

> The revealing feature of Chinese bronze metallurgy lies in the use of its products: the metal was seldom, if ever, used for agricultural production or irrigation; instead, during the Bronze Age the bronze was fashioned into objects that served 'the major affairs of the state,' namely ritual and war. Ritual and war, as the twin instruments of political power, were the keys to the emergence of civilization in ancient China.[9]

THE SEARCH FOR THE XIA DYNASTY

Early writers who described the Xia dynasty (from which the foregoing accounts have been drawn), were suspect because, as historian W. Scott Morton acknowledges, "There was a tendency for the later annalist officials [early historians] to push back as far as possible into the past the appearance of the Chinese state as a centralized, bureaucratic, and dynastic system."[10] Nevertheless, older Chinese scholars, who had high regard for the ancient historians of their country, continued to defend the old records.

A younger, less tradition-bound generation of Chinese historians, however, was growing more and more skeptical. In *Frontiers of Archeology,* author Robert Silverberg says, "They mocked the elaborate genealogies of the ancient monarchs. In a sweeping reaction against the romantic tales of ancient China, these revisionist historians threw all the early dynasties and monarchs under suspicion. Where was the proof? they demanded."[11]

Archaeologists working near the city of Anyang in 1928 discovered proof of the existence of the Shang dynasty, thus restoring a measure of respect for the old texts. However, no evidence for the Xia has yet been found. Some experts do not see this lack of evidence as proof one way or another. The tendency of one dynasty to destroy what its predecessor had built, they say, makes the lack of identifiable ruins unsurprising.

GRAVE ROBBING: AN ARCHAEOLOGICAL TRAGEDY

Many priceless treasures have been stolen or destroyed by looters of ancient Chinese sites. In the past, looters were mainly impoverished peasants willing to risk the wrath of ancestral spirits to find salable treasures. In this excerpt, quoted in Frontiers of Archaeology *by Robert Silverberg, D. H. Creel, an archaeologist who worked at Anyang in 1929, describes how looters operated there, even after a crackdown was initiated by authorities.*

As a result of the official ban on digging, the grave robbers have now developed a method of nocturnal operation. . . . To prevent them from prospecting in the daytime is almost impossible. They use an instrument something like a post hole digger, and when this brings up a peculiar type of 'pounded earth,' they know that they have located an ancient grave. In preparation for digging they assemble fifty or sixty men, all with the greatest secrecy. After nightfall this band, all armed with guns, proceeds to the chosen spot. A few of them dig; the rest, taking advantage of any natural cover, or devising some slight protection, form an armed ring about the scene of operations. Work proceeds feverishly and the entire tomb is gutted before morning. As compared with their abject poverty there is a fortune for each of these peasants at stake in their enterprise. If any attempt is made to interfere with them they will shoot to kill.

This jade knife dates from about 2000 B.C. when the Xia dynasty is thought to have begun.

Many historians continue to hope that physical evidence of the Xia's existence will be unearthed. In the meantime, archaeologists continue to search. During the 1950s through the 1970s a number of early Bronze Age sites identified as the Erlitou culture were excavated in the area around Anyang. Based on the dating and location of these sites, some archaeologists suggest that the Erlitou culture actually may be the long-sought Xia dynasty. According to these researchers, the age of the Erlitou culture (determined by radiocarbon dating) closely matches that traditionally associated with the Xia dynasty.

For the most part, however, this hypothesis has not been accepted among archaeologists because the links are not conclusive. To establish the Xia dynasty's existence beyond question, scholars say the proof must include words, pictographs, or symbols that directly connect the Xia with historical records—the name of a king, perhaps, or description of an event.

Whether such proof will ever be found, even if it exists, is anyone's guess. Historians Caroline Blunden and Mark Elvin comment, "Perhaps the earliest records were written with a brush, in the way that pottery was painted, and kept on materials like wood strips that have now perished, unlike the texts on bone, shell, and bronze from slightly later times."[12]

Nevertheless, many scholars hope that the Xia, like the Shang, eventually will take their place in the historical record. Pure luck may play a part, as it so often has in many other archaeological discoveries. Perhaps a Chinese farmer plowing his field may one day turn up an object that will confirm everything the ancient historians claimed. In the meantime, to account for the fall of the Xia and the rise of the Shang dynasty, reliance must be placed on the ancient texts.

THE FALL OF THE XIA DYNASTY

According to ancient reports, the tranquility brought about by the reigns of Emperors Shaokang and his son Zhu was short-lived. After Zhu died, a succession of self-indulgent tyrants plunged the empire into disarray. Although the shortcomings of the last emperor, Jie, undoubtedly were exaggerated by the Shang to justify his overthrow, stories of his reign make it clear that he was indeed a despot who spent most of his time hunting. He neglected his official duties, except to collect taxes, and he provided farming villages no protection against raiders.

One of Jie's subjects, a man named Tang, was prince of a small kingdom whose farm villages were often raided by nomadic bands. When his appeals to the emperor for protection went unheeded, Tang decided to arm the farmers of his little kingdom and train them to fight. This was a surprising departure from custom, for it was commonly believed that armed peasants were a threat to the ruling family. Nevertheless, Tang took the risk, and because he treated his people justly, he was rewarded with their loyalty.

Now able to defend itself, Tang's little domain grew and prospered. Princes of other kingdoms admired Tang's success, and he began to attract a following. His popularity was also noticed by Emperor Jie, but not with admiration. In fact, Jie planned a secret attack on Tang's domain to be carried out by his own armies and those of an alliance called Kunwu. Word of the impending attack leaked out, however, and Tang was forced to take the initiative. Wu writes:

> A meeting of all Tang's allies and subordinate princes was called; and a united army was speedily raised, with Tang assuming full control and Yi Yin [Tang's friend and adviser] serving as his chief lieutenant. And before Kunwu got wind of what they were doing, they had already crossed the Ji River and destroyed two of its allies in quick succession. The [Kunwu] forces, taken by surprise, were forced to beat a precipitate retreat westward in the direction of the imperial seat, hoping to join with Jie. And Tang followed closely on their heels.[13]

In desperation, Jie assembled an army to meet the advancing troops of Tang and his allies. The ensuing battle was fierce and bloody, but Tang's forces won the day. Emperor Jie and his entourage managed to escape, but no one in the empire would give them sanctuary. When Jie was finally captured, his life was spared and he was allowed to live out his life in exile. Not long afterward (around 1600 B.C.), Tang established the Shang dynasty, sometimes referred to as the Yin, after Tang's adviser. The Shang dynasty would dominate Chinese history for the next five hundred years.

Chapter

2 The Shang Dynasty: Rise of Chinese Civilization

Serendipity—just plain luck—played an important part in the discovery of hard evidence of the Shang dynasty early in the twentieth century. The series of events that led to the discovery actually began in 1899 when Liu Tieyun, a Chinese scholar, was visiting a sick friend in Beijing. His friend was grinding up pieces of tortoiseshell to use in a traditional Chinese remedy when Liu noticed writing on them.

Taking a closer look, he realized that the script on the shell pieces was very much like that on prehistoric bronze urns he had studied. Excited by the possibilities, the two men went to the apothecary shop where the shells had been purchased. The shop owner would not tell them exactly where he had gotten the shells, but he thought the original source was near Anyang, a city southwest of Beijing.

Since archaeology was not well established in China at that time, no official excavations were undertaken at Anyang to locate the source of the shells. However, Liu continued to search the shops for tortoise shell and also for scapula, shoulder blades of large animals used in the same manner as the shells. As his collection grew, Liu published data about his work. His research attracted other scholars who set about deciphering the meaning of the "dragon bones," as they were popularly called.

DECIPHERING THE "DRAGON BONES"

During years of intense study by many Chinese scholars, inscriptions on the tortoise shell and scapula bones were translated and found to be an ancient method of obtaining knowledge about the future. With this discovery, the "dragon bones" became known as oracle bones—bones for predicting future events. Recognizing the vast potential of the bones for unlocking the past, China's first scientific agency, the Academia Sinica (Chinese Academy), sponsored a preliminary search for the source of the bones and shells in 1928.

The search was headed by archaeologist Dong Zuobin, who traced the bones to a mound in a small town near Anyang. Over the next weeks, Dong and a team of six other archaeologists, aided by local workmen, dug up almost eight hundred bones with inscriptions on them. The team became convinced that these finds were just the beginning.

That conviction was justified. In the years that followed, the remains of the lost Shang dynasty were unearthed, including cities, tombs, and thousands of additional oracle shells and bones. More than mere curiosities, the oracle bones contained the earliest writing ever found in China. They revealed the names of kings, dates of events, and provided tantalizing glimpses of life in the Shang dynasty.

The subsequent unearthing of royal tombs and other Shang ruins by professional archaeologists supported the testi-

Excavations in the late 1920s uncovered the remains of royal tombs, whose contents helped archaeologists understand what life was like during the Shang dynasty.

mony of the oracle bones. The digs and the bones together unveiled a powerful dynasty in which life was luxurious for the ruling elite but harsh and violent for the common people.

POLITICAL AND MILITARY ORGANIZATION

The Shang empire consisted of a large number of clans, perhaps two or three hundred. The dominant clan was the Shang, headed by a king who wielded great power. Maintaining control required constant vigilance, however. Subordinate clans with ambitions of their own posed an unceasing threat to Shang rulers. The oracle bones reveal that the dynastic capital was moved several times, indicating political unrest within the empire.

Archaeologist Kwang-chih Chang writes, "Bronze Age China was a vast sea of many thousands or tens of thousands of towns and villages, organized into many hundreds or tens of hundreds of networks that the Chinese call *guo* (states or kingdoms)."[14] These small kingdoms, founded by members of various clans, were intensely competitive and thus a threat to political stability.

How Shang rulers maintained control over such an empire is explained by Kwang-chih Chang: "Younger brothers and nephews of the king were sometimes sent off to establish junior statelets to colonize the vast and sparsely populated territories between existing states and to serve as satellite polities to support and guard the cities of their kings."[15]

THE WRITTEN WORD

The Chinese writing system probably began as pictographs (simple pictures of the objects in question) and progressively developed into more complex figures (ideograms and logographs) to express ideas. In the excerpts here, taken from China: Its History and Culture, *author W. Scott Morton explains the development and importance of written Chinese.*

It is certain that the Chinese form of writing is an entirely distinct and native product. Chinese script appears about 1300 B.C. . . . on the oracle bones discovered chiefly at Anyang, the later Shang capital. These bones were found in large numbers and therefore form a significant sample for the study of the evolving Chinese language. . . .

The important points for the historian in all this are, first, that the script on the bones is clearly the ancestor of modern Chinese and essentially the same in character structure [word form], and second, that the written language, when it first appears in Shang times, is already developed and no longer primitive. . . . The basic idea is the representation of objects by pictures, pictograms. Other peoples, such as those of ancient Egypt and the North American Indian tribes, also used this method. But before the Anyang period of Shang the Chinese had taken the decisive step forward of combining pictures to represent abstract ideas, as in the character 'to pray' . . . a man kneeling before a divine symbol. Here a pictogram becomes an ideogram, and the Chinese language is launched upon a developing course of infinite variety and richness.

Written Chinese, moreover, acts as a cultural bond between those in different regions of the country who have come in the course of time to speak mutually incomprehensible dialects. It is also a unifying factor for all of East Asia, between China and the peripheral areas which have borrowed her culture: Korea, Japan, Vietnam, Tibet, and Mongolia. Throughout all the changes which the language has undergone, rich overtones of an aesthetic and spiritual nature still dwell in written Chinese and add immeasurably to its artistic and literary appeal. 'Leisure,' for instance, is represented by moonlight through the opening of a door, and 'good' by the picture of a woman and child.

By such means, the Shang dynasty lasted for over five hundred years (1600–1050 B.C.), during which at least thirty kings reigned. Their names and dates were deciphered from the oracle bones and found to be nearly identical to a list compiled in the first century B.C. by historian Sima Qian.

As was true of earlier rulers, the military superiority of Shang kings came from bronze, both from its production and from manufactured bronze objects, particularly

BRONZE PIECE-MOLD CASTING

The superb quality of bronze objects, particularly wine vessels and food servers, is undoubtedly the greatest distinction of the Shang dynasty. Never before or since have bronze artisans reached the level of workmanship displayed on objects attributed to the Shang and their successors, the Zhou. In this excerpt from The Great Bronze Age of China, *edited by Wen Fong, Ma Chengyuan, curator of the Shanghai Museum, describes the way such pieces were made.*

Many unearthed relics verify that in casting Shang dynasty bronze objects, ceramic piece molds were used. Based on extensive research on ceramic molds, we can outline the piece-mold process. First a model of the bronze vessel to be cast was sculpted from high quality clay. Then, following the necessary divisions, pieces of molds were pressed onto the surface of the model. Mortises and tenons [fasteners] were made on the pieces of the mold to join them. The broad decor of the design was carved on the model and transferred to the mold, on which the finer details were added. Thereafter a surface layer was shaved from the clay model. The portion removed would exactly represent the thickness of the cast-bronze vessel, and the remaining clay model became the inner core. After the outer and inner parts of the clay model assembly were dried, they were fired to form ceramic molds. The bronze casters had only to join the pieces of the mold together according to the fit of the mortises and tenons. Then the molten bronze could be poured into a hole left for that purpose. When the bronze was cool, the mold was removed and with some filing and polishing the bronze vessel became an excellent cast-bronze object. The greatest advantage of casting bronze vessels with ceramic piece molds lies in the superb clarity that one can achieve on the cast article; ceramic molds are capable of reproducing exquisite craftsmanship and delicate precision.

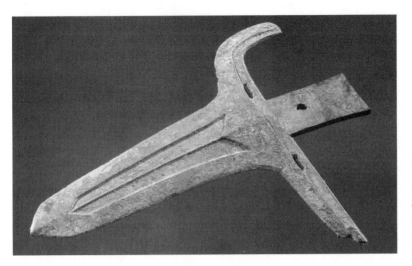

Bronze weapons used by the Shang nobility during war gave them a decisive advantage over their enemies, who lacked such weapons.

weapons. "The possession of bronze weapons," historians Caroline Blunden and Mark Elvin write ". . . gave those who were privileged to have them a nearly decisive superiority in the use of force. We may surmise that this ensured both the dominance of a warrior nobility of clan leaders over their commoners, and of the Shang people as a whole over the less advanced tribes who lived around and among them."[16]

Shang kings waged continuous war to keep overly ambitious clans under control, to protect their own borders from attack, and most importantly, to expand the empire. Offensive military campaigns not only increased Shang territory but enriched the dynasty with loot and tribute from conquered tribes. War was also useful for obtaining slaves as laborers or for sacrifices in Shang religious rituals.

Warfare was highly organized and led by an elite military corps that was trained on elaborate big-game hunting expeditions. Shang army units included horse and elephant cavalry, foot soldiers, arch-ers, and for the first time in Chinese history, horse-drawn chariots. Whether chariots were adopted from other peoples or invented independently in China is unknown, but their impact on the Shang's enemies was devastating.

Sudden assaults on villages and towns by charioteers wielding bronze weapons revolutionized warfare. The Stone Age weapons of Shang foes were no match against bronze halberds (long-handled axes), arrowheads, and spear points. Robert Silverberg imagines how such a raid might have taken place: "Terrifying bronze-helmeted warriors roared through the towns, drawn in chariots by fierce, snarling horses and perhaps backed up by a heavy cavalry of elephants. It would have been no contest."[17]

Of course, bronze arms and armor were only for the upper ranks of the Shang military. Allowing hordes of common soldiers to possess metal weapons was too risky for the ruling clan. Besides, it was unnecessary. A few bronze weapons in the hands of small, well-trained units were

AN OBSESSION WITH HUNTING

As the following two excerpts attest, big game hunting was a very popular pastime for aristocrats and military officers of Shang society. The first excerpt is from Cultural Atlas of China *by Caroline Blunden and Mark Elvin and the second from* Frontiers in Archeology *by Robert Silverberg.*

The new [bronze] weapons may also have been part of the explanation of the passion of the Shang aristocrats for hunting. The kings maintained a huge hunting ground on the western skirts of the Tai and Meng mountains in the southern part of what is now Shangdong province. Excavations of Shang sites have yielded the bones of elephants, rhinoceroses, bears, tigers, leopards, deer, monkeys, foxes, and badgers. The hunting meet was also the best training for battle. Individuals could practice the use of weapons, and groups the art of moving in coordination.

* * * * *

We know that the Shang nobles were great hunters. The excavations at Anyang unearthed the remains of many wild animals from monkeys to whales. . . . That these were taken by Shang hunters is proven by the numerous oracular inscriptions having to do with prospects for the chase:

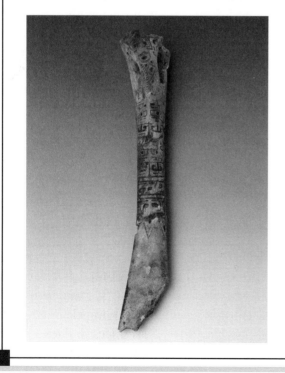

> Divine on the day *Wu-wu, Ku* [the diviner] made the inquiry, we are going to hunt at *Ch'iu,* any capture?
> Hunting on this day, we actually captured:
> Tigers, one
> Deer, forty
> Foxes, one hundred and sixty four
> Hornless deer, one hundred and fifty nine.

Aristocrats during the Shang dynasty were avid hunters, as indicated by the bones that were discovered strewn around Shang excavation sites.

sufficient to rout enemies lacking such weapons. Moreover, populations were large, offering an endless supply of troops. No matter how many soldiers were killed, a king could always conscript more.

A Shang king's leadership depended on more than just political savvy or military prowess. Intertwined with a king's political and military duties were his duties as chief spiritual leader, a role that entailed the awesome responsibility of appeasing royal ancestors.

RELIGIOUS BELIEFS AND RITUALS

Like that of the Xia before them, the major religious system of the Shang was ancestor worship, based on the belief that, after death, life continued in a spirit world in much the same manner as in the real world. More importantly, the deceased did not just withdraw into the spirit world, but were believed to have power over the living. This power could be helpful or harmful depending upon how well living descendants honored their ancestors through offerings, homage, and sacrifices.

The most important facet of ancestor worship affecting the empire as a whole was the king's relationship with the spirit world. Kings were believed to be descended from Di, the high god in heaven, thereby legitimizing their right to rule. However, this right also carried obligations. Decisions made by Shang kings and actions taken by them in the real world had to be based on the wishes of royal ancestors. Historian Patricia Buckley Ebrey explains:

The Shang king played a priestly role in the worship of the high god Di and the royal ancestors, a role that justified his political powers. To put this another way, it was because among the dead his ancestors were best able to communicate with Di and because among the living he was best able to communicate with his ancestors that the king was fitted to rule.[18]

Shang kings, therefore, spent a great deal of time divining ancestors' wishes by means of oracle bones. Apparently, the wishes of ancestral spirits included human sacrifice and thus, from the king's perspective, it was a necessity. His own well-being as well as that of the empire depended on it. Carrying out the grim rituals with suitable pomp and ceremony was important, too. Magnificent bronze wine and food containers were created by Shang artisans expressly for such occasions. The political and social importance of these pieces is explained by Ma Chengyuan, curator of the Shanghai Museum:

Other important objects cast in bronze [in addition to weapons] were the ritual vessels, which indicated the status of their users and their exclusive right to perform sacrifices and ritual ceremonies. These vessels included cooking vessels, food vessels, wine containers, wine-drinking vessels, and washing vessels. The clan structure of the Shang-Zhou ruling class especially emphasized sacrifices to the ancestors, and those sacrifices required a large number of implements.[19]

Elaborate cooking vessels were constructed of bronze and used for solemn ceremonies like ritual sacrifice.

The victims in these terrifying rituals were varied. Both males and females were sacrificed, children as well as adults. Some victims, such as concubines of kings and princes, were of high status. More often they were servants or slaves. Whoever the victims were, their purpose was to serve their masters in the spirit world. Animals were sacrificed, too—dogs, in particular, but even wild beasts such as rhinoceroses and elephants. Horses were often buried along with the chariots they pulled and the charioteers who drove them.

The numbers of victims in a tomb ranged from only a few to dozens or even hundreds. "Life was cheap in Shang China," Silverberg observes, "and ritual terror must have been a part of everyday existence. . . . In one season alone at Anyang, the excavators came upon a thousand headless victims of Shang sacrifices."[20]

Although it would have been small consolation to the victims, sacrificial rituals actually touched only a small portion of the empire's large population. Away from the seats of power, people went about the business of living as they had done for centuries. Ebrey observes, "Ancient China was populated by more than kings, warriors, diviners, and bronzesmiths. The vast majority of the population, then and later, were farmers, toiling in their fields, trying to fashion satisfying lives and to limit the exactions [demands] of those with power over them."[21]

SOCIAL AND ECONOMIC INSTITUTIONS

Grand though the Shang dynasty might have been, simple farmers toiling in the fields made that grandeur possible. The Shang economy still rested largely on an agricultural foundation not far advanced from that of the preceding Neolithic Age. Some progressive steps had been made, such as domestication of water buffalo, but the use of metal farm tools was rare, as most farmers were too poor to afford them.

This economic and technological lag is not surprising, as cultural changes of this magnitude are never abrupt. What is surprising is that the Shang empire endured for so long supported only by agriculture. This was due in part to intelligent management at the top. Most Shang kings were able administrators, or at least were served by capable subordinates. Many attributes associated with civilization were present in Shang society, including trade with other peoples, a money system, a calendar, metallurgy, standardized measurements, and a system of writing.

However, it was the enormous workforce at the bottom—thousands of conscripted laborers and slaves who spent their entire lives constructing tombs, palaces, fortifications, and gigantic public works—that sustained the Shang dynasty for so long. Commenting on these massive projects, Ebrey writes, "The enormous city walls of Zhengzhou [a Shang capital city], which were 60 feet wide, 30 feet high, and 2,385 feet long would have taken ten to twenty years to complete,

even with 10,000 labourers working to move and ram the earth."[22]

Despite the large number of workers such projects required, historians Blunden and Elvin are not convinced that slavery was the basis of the Shang economy:

It is of course probable that some of the population were slaves. . . . But it seems unlikely that the system of production as a whole was based on slavery. There is no evidence of any regular procurement [of slaves], and war would have been too chancy a basis for an entire economy. . . . It is more likely . . . that the temporary conscription of subordinate kin-groups provided the labor for tomb construction, as it did for other services, and it is fairly certain that the majority of those murdered to accompany funerals were non-Chinese prisoners of war.[23]

Armed with bronze weapons like the head of this battle ax, small groups of Shang dynasty soldiers could easily rout their enemies.

Whether the function of slaves was principally for labor or sacrifice, there was an unbridgeable distance between their position in Shang society and the upper end of the social structure, where a privileged elite lived in comfort and splendor. Sumptuous palaces, elaborate underground tombs, and art treasures made of jade and bronze were the outward symbols of wealth and power among the Shang.

PALACES, TOMBS, AND ART TREASURES

Because Shang palaces were made of wood and other perishable materials, none have survived intact. In all probability, however, they were destroyed long before decay set in, as it was the policy of conquering armies to completely demolish the buildings of their enemies. What did survive, however, are building foundations and a few other traces that yield clues to the appearance of Shang structures.

Foundations were made of rammed earth, a building technique in which dirt is tamped down and packed so tightly it becomes almost like concrete. In excavations, rammed earth can easily be distinguished from regular soil, enabling archaeologists to determine the dimensions and layouts of the original buildings.

For instance, in 1931, when the first digs were just getting underway at Anyang, archaeologists found the remains of what seemed to be part of a royal enclave. The outlines of fifteen dwellings were discovered, with foundations of rammed earth ten feet thick. Resting on these foundations were rows of huge stones on which wooden pillars probably were erected to hold up the roof.

Although the appearance of Shang palaces can only be imagined today, hundreds of Shang tombs of varying richness have been discovered and excavated since the diggings at Anyang began in the late 1920s. Most had been plundered by grave robbers long before archaeologists arrived, but the general structure of the tombs was still intact. The building of a tomb began with the digging of a huge pit such as those found at Anyang in 1934 and described by the authors of *China's Buried Kingdoms:*

> When each of the great kings who had been buried here died, a great pit was dug; the largest measured almost 58 feet long, 53 feet wide at the mouth, and 39 feet deep. Earth from such pits was brought out along the ramps that had been cut in the sides. At the bottom of the shaft, a smaller pit was carved out of the soil. Around the sides a ledge of pounded earth was made, and a wooden chamber, some eight feet high, built on it. The coffin containing the dead king was installed inside, surrounded by royal grave goods. The chamber was then closed with a roof of elaborately carved and painted timbers and earth laid on top.[24]

As archaeologists explored the recesses of these royal tombs, they found evidence

THE TREASURE-FILLED TOMB OF A SHANG QUEEN

Until recent times, Fu Hao, a favorite wife of Shang king Wu Ding, was known only from inscriptions on oracle bones. From the bones, it was clear that she was a remarkable woman in an age when women were rarely heard from. In 1976, while digging near the city of Anyang, archaeologists were astonished to discover her unplundered tomb. In the following excerpt from the Cambridge Illustrated History of China, *author Patricia Buckley Ebrey describes this amazing tomb and the woman who occupied it.*

Lady Hao's tomb, unearthed in 1976, housed the most complete collection of Shang bronze vessels ever found.

The only royal Shang tomb never to have been robbed before it was excavated is tomb 5 at Anyang for Lady Hao (c. 1250 BC). One of the smaller tombs (about 13 by 18 feet at the mouth and about 25 feet deep), and not in the main royal cemetery, it was nonetheless filled with an extraordinary array of sacrificial goods.

Human sacrifice is evident (the sixteen human skeletons include both males and females, children and adults), but not on as great a scale as some of the larger tombs. Rather it is the burial of a profusion of valuable objects that is the most striking feature of this burial. . . . In this tomb were 460 bronze objects (including more than 130 weapons, 23 bells, 27 knives, 4 mirrors, and 4 tigers or tiger heads), nearly 750 jade objects, some 70 stone sculptures, nearly 500 bone hairpins, over 20 bone arrowheads, and 3 ivory carvings. In addition, there were nearly 6,900 cowry shells, possibly evidence that these shells were used for money. . . .

The 200-odd bronze vessels constitute the largest and most complete set of ritual vessels unearthed from a Shang grave. . . . Vessels for holding wine predominate, suggesting that as a last step at the funeral ceremonies mourners made a libation [drink] of wine and tossed in the wine cup as well as the wine. Some sixty bronze vessels have Lady Hao's name inscribed on them.

The artefacts in the tomb do not provide much evidence of what Lady Hao was like as a person. Probably she is the same Lady Hao mentioned in many oracle bone inscriptions as one of the many wives of the King Wu Ding (c. 1200 BC). The king made divinations concerning her illnesses and pregnancies. From these inscriptions we also know that she took charge of certain rituals and had a landed estate outside the capital. She even led military campaigns, once with 13,000 troops against the Qiang to the west, at other times against the Fu Fang in the northwest, the Ba Fang in the southwest, and the Yi in the east.

of numerous ritual sacrifices. In one tomb alone, 17 men, 24 women, 16 charioteers, 16 chariot horses, 8 dogs, and 34 human skulls were discovered. Most of what would be considered treasure had disappeared from these tombs, but in 1976, archaeologists were gratified to find an unplundered royal Shang tomb, that of Fu Hao, a remarkable Shang queen, whose relatively small tomb contained hundreds of artifacts, among them beautiful bronze and jade objects fashioned by Shang artisans.

JADE CARVING AND BRONZE CASTING

Beautiful jade objects have been found in great numbers, not only in Shang sites, but in many of the ruins of late Neolithic cultures preceding the Shang. Jade is an extremely hard stone produced under tremendous pressure. Unlike marble and other less dense rocks, it cannot be carved or sculpted. Rather it must be laboriously shaped by sawing, filing, and grinding with abrasives to produce the desired objects.

While beautifully crafted jade objects are associated with the Shang, it is their work in bronze that is the defining characteristic of their society. Jade carving was already an old art in Shang times, but Shang bronzes were unprecedented and unsurpassed. Historian Christopher Hibbert comments, "Their bronzes were among the finest masterpieces of early Chinese civilization, comparable to the greatest works of the European Renaissance. (In Greece and the Near East, bronze casting began in about 2500 B.C.—but nowhere rivaled Shang proficiency.)"[25]

The bronze castings by artisans during the Shang period constitute some of the finest work in bronze in the history of civilization.

Numerous bronze bells have been recovered at various Shang burial sites. These bells did not have clappers, but were sounded by striking them with wooden poles.

Bronze is an alloy of copper and tin. Its very existence in Shang society implies an advanced knowledge of metallurgy, including methods for mining, extracting, and smelting ores; transport of the ores to distant work sites; experimentation to produce alloys; and techniques of casting.

Other societies around the world had mastered these processes long before the Shang dynasty existed. What sets Shang artisans apart, however, is their ability to flawlessly cast bronze into intricate shapes and patterns. An unsolved mystery is how they attained such perfection so quickly. Archaeologists expected to find bronze artifacts demonstrating a gradual development of the art, but so far, very little evidence of such a progression has turned up.

Shang bronzes were cast by the piece-mold method, which entails assembly of separate pieces after casting. The object to be cast was first modeled in clay; then sectional ceramic molds were made from the clay model. The mold sections were then fitted together (with a solid ceramic core inside) and molten bronze was poured into the space between the mold and the core. When cooled, the mold sections were taken away and the completed piece removed. Several separate castings were necessary for some of the more intricate pieces.

The bulk of bronze objects produced by the Shang (of which hundreds have been recovered) were ritual pieces used in sacred rites and ceremonies. Much more rarely, archaeologists find musical instruments made of bronze. For example, a cylindrical drum weighing ninety-three pounds was recovered in Hubei Province (central China) in 1977. It rests horizontally on a bronze base so that both ends could be beaten. Its outside surface is decorated with intricate scrollwork.

Musical bells dating to the Shang period have also been found. A large bronze bell discovered in Hunan Province (south central China) in 1959 weighs 338 pounds. Its surface is richly decorated with scrolls and geometric patterns. Inside the bell, near the rim, are two tiny bronze tigers. Bells such as these had no clappers. Judging from designs appearing on other bronze artwork, the bells were struck on the outside with wooden poles to produce tones. Since only the wealthy could afford such instruments, they were used in important ceremonies for the enjoyment of the elite. It is also known that large bells were sounded in battles as a signal to retreat.

Since bronze vessels were proof of wealth and power, Chinese legends say that certain objects were passed down through the ages as royal standards, much like the crown jewels of other monarchies. Kwang-chih describes such a legend:

> The political importance of the bronzes is well expressed by the legend of the Nine Bronze Tripods [three-footed vessel]. It says that Yu, founder of the Xia dynasty, cast the Nine Tripods, which became the symbols of political legitimacy. When the Xia dynasty fell, the Nine Tripods were transferred to the Shang. The Shang in their turn lost these symbols of legitimate power, along with their political mandate, to the succeeding Zhou Dynasty.[26]

THE END OF THE SHANG DYNASTY

The success of the Shang dynasty eventually became its undoing. For example, the economy was weakened by the extravagance of its ruling classes and their insatiable demands for luxurious palaces, expensive furnishings, personal adornment, and pleasurable pursuits. Equally unrestrained in death, emperors and other elite society members spent fortunes building their final resting places.

The dynasty was also weakened militarily by wars of expansion and by defense measures taken against hostile border tribes. Civil unrest also took its toll as the dynasty's overburdened and overtaxed subjects grew more and more rebellious. The circumstance that finally tipped the scale against the dynasty, however, was the decadence of the last emperor and his sadistic empress who, according to Chinese historians, devised excruciating tortures for those who failed to show proper respect to the emperor.

The Shang dynasty was overthrown by the Zhou, one of its own vassal states. Around 1050 B.C., Zhou armies under the leadership of Wu Wang, which translates as King Wu, overthrew their Shang masters while the main Shang army was waging a military campaign away from the capital. Joined by other clans hostile to the Shang, the Zhou were triumphant. The last Shang king, Di-Xin, died in flames in his own palace as rebels stormed the capital city, Anyang.

Chapter

3 The Western (Early) Zhou Dynasty: Peaceful Interlude

The Zhou dynasty is the longest dynasty in Chinese history. However, the early centuries are so different from the later ones that historians divide it into two distinct phases, based on time and the location of its capital. During the Early or Western Zhou (1050–771 B.C.), the capital was at Xian. During the Late or Eastern Zhou (771–256 B.C.), the capital was moved east to Luoyang. The first phase is noted for its relative peace and tranquility, the second for unceasing conflict.

The Zhou kingdom lay on the western border of the Shang empire, about three hundred miles southwest of Anyang, the Shang capital. Perhaps a seminomadic pastoral people at an earlier stage, by the eleventh century B.C. the Zhou were firmly settled. According to accounts written during the Zhou and the later Han dynasties, early Zhou leaders were capable men who governed wisely and built up a prosperous kingdom.

The most revered of these leaders was Wen Wang, who was also known as the cultural king. He was described as a good and just ruler who cared about his people. He was also very ambitious and had been planning the conquest of the Shang years

before he and his son actually accomplished it. Oracle bone inscriptions show that he made sacrifices to Shang ancestors, which suggests that he was a dutiful vassal, but the inscriptions also show that he could be troublesome. Robert W. Bagley writes:

> Wen Wang's loyalty . . . was more than a little doubtful. By rights he was entitled to call himself an earl, but the oracle inscriptions from Qishan [a Shang city] prove that he was called Wen Wang not only by posterity [future generations], but also in his own lifetime, and this use of the title *wang*, 'king,' amounts to open usurpation of the Shang king's prerogatives [exclusive rights]. . . . Wen Wang's move eastward to found a new capital at Xi'an, on the borders of the Shang state, seems equally ominous. The Shang king must no doubt have felt it so.[27]

THE ZHOU DYNASTY BEGINS

The Shang king had good reason to worry. Around 1050 B.C., Wen Wang's son,

Wu Wang, toppled the Shang dynasty, ending its reign of more than five hundred years. Overthrowing the Shang dynasty was simple, however, compared with the next step—extending Zhou rule over the vast empire. By the time the Shang fell, their territory stretched hundreds of miles westward from the seacoast across north China, encompassing large portions of the Yellow and Yangtze River valleys.

Wu Wang was equal to the task. Like his father, he was considered a good and just ruler, not only politically but in domestic matters as well. He stressed the importance of family obligations, insisting that all family members show respect for one another. He hated drunkenness and, except for religious rituals, tried to discourage communal wine drinking. He is also known for his emphasis on the equal administration of justice.

Faced with the awesome task of controlling the old Shang empire, Wu Wang instituted a kind of feudal system of government; that is, he ruled through a network of nobles who owed their positions and wealth to his own influence. Historian Patricia Buckley Ebrey writes:

> Rather than attempt to control all of their territories directly, the early Zhou rulers sent out relatives and trusted subordinates with troops to establish walled garrisons in the conquered territories. Where that was not possible, they recognized local chiefs as their representatives. These lords were given titles that became heredi-

tary and were obliged to render military service and send tribute.[28]

Some historians doubt that the Zhou established a feudal system in the strictest sense of the term. There is no doubt, however, that the Zhou empire was highly decentralized, with numerous officials in influential positions far from the center of power. For example, to discourage possible Shang uprisings, Wu Wang divided the Shang state into three parts. He installed his brother, the duke of Zhou, over one part, and appointed two more brothers to head the other parts. Unfortunately, Wu Wang's tremendous task of consolidating the empire was left unfinished when he died about seven years after the conquest.

THE DUKE OF ZHOU BECOMES REGENT

Because Wu Wang's son was too young to assume the throne immediately following his father's death, Wu's brother, the duke of Zhou, was appointed regent (temporary ruler) until his nephew came of age. The duke's other brothers immediately assumed he was going to take over the dynasty for himself. Accordingly, they plotted an insurrection against him, assisted by some members of the vanquished Shang dynasty.

Saddened that he was forced to act against his own brothers, the duke of Zhou nevertheless firmly put down the uprising. When defeat for the rebels was imminent, the duke's older brother, the

A Powerful Regent Willingly Steps Down

Probably no other person in Chinese history is more respected than the duke of Zhou. When his brother King Wu died, the duke became regent for Wu's young son, Cheng Wang. Believing the duke had designs on the throne, other brothers rose up against him. He put down the rebellion and in the end proved them wrong about his intentions. From traditional Chinese literary sources, K. C. Wu reconstructs the dramatic story of Cheng Wang's coronation in his book The Chinese Heritage.

Then came the seventh year of the regency. As soon as the year was over, according to the customary Chinese computation, Cheng Wang would be adjudged of age, fully twenty years old. It was therefore the regent's intention to return full sovereignty to his nephew just before the end of the year. For this purpose, he journeyed again to the new capital, and saw to it that all the construction works, especially the Bright Hall and the imperial palace, be completed in time, to the very last of the finishing touches. [He then invited all the princes and chieftains to attend the coronation ceremony, and on the appointed day, Cheng Wang came to the new capital city.]

On arrival, he first sacrificed to Wen Wang [his grandfather] and Wu Wang [his father], using a red-haired ox for each. Then he worshipped Heaven and other deities. And finally, at the appointed time, after all the princes and chieftains had assembled at their predesignated places, he appeared at the Bright Hall. Standing at the center of the raised altar under a red silk umbrella bordered with rare black feathers, he faced to the south and started receiving homage. And whom did the 1,800 and some princes and chieftains present behold leading the procession, doing obeisance to the sovereign, and offering to him their insignias for verification and confirmation but the regent [the duke of Zhou] and Taigong! [a famous general]. While these princes and Chieftains following the lead, were each going through the same ceremonials, they could not help casting glances on the man who had just relinquished the supreme power of the world he had held so resolutely and so indomitably these last seven years, and who was now stationing himself along with some others in front of the altar. And, in truth, as they watched to see how he was deporting himself, the duke was in every respect looking as attentive, as reverential, as fearful of the majesty of the young sovereign as the humblest among themselves.

prince of Guan, hanged himself. His two younger brothers were taken alive. One of them, the prince of Cai, was put under house arrest, and the other, the prince of Huo, was stripped of his titles and made a commoner.

The duke then destroyed the old Shang capital at Anyang, and redivided the Shang state, this time into two parts. Over one part he placed a trusted member of the Shang royal family. "The remainder of the Shang domain," Bagley states, "was given to another brother of the duke of Zhou, Kang Hou; Wu Wang's supply of brothers seems to have been inexhaustible."[29]

The duke of Zhou then continued the job of consolidating the empire, which involved a two-year struggle against tribes of barbarians who had joined forces with the Shang rebels. (Barbarian was a term used at the time by settled peoples in China to identify nomadic tribes, whom they considered less advanced than themselves.) By such actions during his term as

The Zhou continued to make elaborate objects in bronze, such as this model of a carriage.

regent, the duke of Zhou gained great personal power and respect from his subjects.

Nevertheless, when it came time for his nephew, Cheng Wang, to assume the throne, the duke of Zhou graciously stepped aside. "The admiration expressed by historians for this virtuous deed borders on astonishment," comments Bagley. "The duke of Zhou became a paragon [ideal] for the moralists of later centuries."[30]

ZHOU SOCIAL STRUCTURE

Although honorable rulers (such as the upright duke of Zhou) undoubtedly made life more tolerable for the common people, the Zhou dynasty remained a highly stratified society with a great gulf between the haves and have-nots. At the top of the social structure, of course, was the royal family, to whom the lords of the domains gave their allegiance. Ebrey describes the Zhou social system:

> By 800 BC there were around two hundred lords with domains large and small, of which only about twenty-five were large enough to matter much. Each lord appointed various officers under him, men with ritual, administrative, or military responsibilities, and these posts and the associated titles tended to become hereditary as well. In this way each domain came to have aristocratic families with patrimonies [entitlements] in offices and associated lands. Society was conceived in strongly hierarchical terms ranging from the Son of Heaven, through the lords, to the great ministers, other officers, the knights and court attendants, and finally the ordinary farmers who generally seem to have been attached to domains in a serf-like manner.[31]

Slavery still existed, too, although not as prominently as during the Shang dynasty. Nevertheless, in spite of rigid class distinctions, there are numerous indications that the extravagance and severity of the Shang kings was considerably softened during the Western Zhou period. Historians Caroline Blunden and Mark Elvin comment, "The extravagance of the Shang, its great hunts and sacrificial murders, gave way to a relative restraint, though both of these practices continued."[32]

Descriptions of Western Zhou rulers, particularly in the dynasty's first few decades, contrast so markedly with accounts of the vain, extravagant, and often sadistic rulers of the previous dynasty that they seem almost unbelievable. Skeptics point to the fact that most of the glowing reports come from Zhou and Han dynasty historians. No historical accounts from the conquered Shang have survived. Accordingly, Blunden and Elvin add a word of caution:

> There is reason to be skeptical about many aspects of the rosy traditional picture. The Zhou were the first masters of political propaganda in China. They probably destroyed the literature of the Shang (none of which has survived in a form that is certainly authentic), lest it support a view of

history different from their own. They certainly set about preaching an ingenious and persuasive doctrine to reconcile the conquered Shang to their subjection.[33]

A New Religious Doctrine

The "ingenious and persuasive doctrine" referred to by Blunden and Elvin consisted of a new concept that the Zhou grafted onto traditional ancestor worship practiced by the Shang. Although it was still necessary for the king to appease ancestral spirits, Zhou theologians taught that making sacrifices was not enough. For the kingdom to survive, moral fitness was required of kings and their ruling houses. Moreover, rulers were constrained to govern justly and display genuine concern for their subjects. If they failed to meet these standards, warnings would be given from above through omens and natural disasters. If the warnings went unheeded, the rule of the kingdom would be taken away and given to those who were worthy of it.

According to Zhou theologians, this is exactly what happened to the Xia and Shang dynasties. Their kings had grown corrupt, depraved, and unfit to reign. Thus, the so-called mandate of heaven, the right to rule, was removed from them and their destruction was a punishment sent from heaven.

Although this new concept was undoubtedly a way for the Zhou kings to justify their rebellion against the Shang, the fact that they felt justification was necessary was a notable departure from past ways of thinking. Bagley says, "The Zhou rationale for imperial legitimacy . . . clearly implies that the right to rule is dependent upon the morality of the ruling house—a claim that it would not have occurred to a Shang king to make."[34] This change in philosophy, that rulers must be moral or pay the price, became an important tenet in Chinese thought from the Western Zhou dynasty onward.

Although a great deal of documented Chinese history is devoted to the worship of ancestral spirits through divining and sacrificial offerings, these practices involved only the elite members of Zhou society, a tiny fraction of the population. Historian W. Scott Morton explains what the common people were doing while their rulers were appeasing the spirits with food, wine, and sacrifices:

> It should be emphasized, that the common people had no part in the ceremonies of ancestor worship, which were reserved for the families of the gentry. . . . The common folk in China did not even have surnames, much less recorded ancestors. . . . The religion of the peasant farmer was marked by worship of the local deities of the soil, and of fertility, and by shamanistic cults involving spirit mediums, exorcists or sorcerers called *wu*, who danced in frenzy.[35]

Except for new concepts in the religious sphere (which probably were important only to royalty), everyday life in the Early Zhou dynasty did not change significantly at first from life under the Shang.

As vassals of the Shang (and semibarbarian ones, at that), the Zhou had absorbed the more refined culture of the Shang and saw no reason to depart from it. Over time, however, changes involving agriculture, economics, and fine arts began to clearly distinguish the Zhou dynasty from that of the Shang.

SOCIAL AND CULTURAL CHANGES

Important advances were made in agriculture during the Early Zhou period, among them the beginning of crop rotation to increase production, and the introduction of soybeans, a versatile crop that provided food for both humans and animals. A very important step forward occurred in metallurgy with the appearance of cast iron tools and weapons, an innovation that became particularly significant in the later, war-torn era of the Zhou dynasty. In bronze metallurgy, there was very little difference at first between Shang bronzes and those of Early Zhou artisans. Gradually, however, many Zhou pieces took on a different character involving the use of inscriptions.

Some of the Shang bronzes had very brief inscriptions on them, usually only the name of the owner. During the Western Zhou era, the inscriptions began to grow much longer until some bronzes were mainly a medium for a message. It seems not to have mattered whether the object itself was well made. Of these bronze pieces Bagley comments, "At times we receive the impression that, for the Zhou nobleman, bronze casting was merely the most prestigious form of publication."[36]

The messages on the bronzes mainly concerned important events in the lives of those who owned them, but also included additional historical information, such as the names and dates of kings and other officials whom the owners or their ancestors had served. For instance, a large cache of Early Zhou bronze pieces was discovered in the 1970s in the area around the original Zhou capital of Xian. Among them was an urn cast in the first year of Wu Wang's

Bronze objects during the Zhou dynasty bore lengthy inscriptions mainly dealing with events in the lives of their owners.

HISTORY WRITTEN IN BRONZE

In 1980 the People's Republic of China in cooperation with the Metropolitan Museum of Art in New York City brought a traveling exhibition of Chinese bronze artwork to the United States. Included in the collection was a bronze urn dating to the beginning of the Western Zhou dynasty. Aside from its value as an artistic piece, the urn is priceless for its lengthy inscription, described below by Robert W. Bagley in The Great Bronze Age of China, *edited by Wen Fong.*

The inscription of the *zun* [type of urn] . . . gives an exact date for the event it describes, in the fifth year of Cheng Wang. The occasion was the king's audience with one of his retainers, a man named He. He, possibly accompanied by members of his clan, was honored with a moral homily [sermon], after which the king made him a present of money in the form of cowrie shells. The money was afterwards used by He to cast the vessel that commemorates the occasion.

[*Bagley then quotes the inscription that He placed upon the urn.*] It was at the time when the king began the building of Cheng Zhou [a city], and offered a Fu sacrifice in the hall of Heaven to (his father) Wu Wang. In the fourth month, on the day *bing xu*, the king was in the Jing Hall and exhorted me saying, "In days past, your late ancestor Gong Shi was able to serve Wen Wang. Wen Wang accepted the great command, and Wu Wang carried out the conquest of the Great City of Shang, announcing it to Heaven with the words, 'I must dwell in the center, and from there rule the people.' Now take heed! You must cherish the memory of the services that Gong Shi rendered to Heaven. Sacrifice to him with reverence!" Our king has indeed a virtuous character, compliant to Heaven, an inspiring example to my own feebleness. When the king had concluded, I, He, was given thirty strings of cowries, which I have used to make this vessel for sacrifices to Gong Shi. This happened in the king's fifth year.

Wealthy nobles in the Zhou era often used bronze items to publicize important events in their lives.

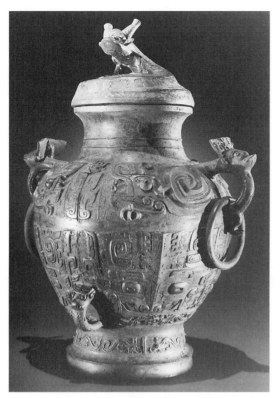

Bronze pieces cast during the Zhou dynasty employed distinctive decorations as well as unusual forms.

reign. The inscription on it says (among many other things) that Wu Wang banished the Shang; that the urn was commissioned by a man named Li eight days after the conquest; that Li was honored by Wu Wang for a service he rendered the king; and that the urn's purpose was for sacrifices to Li's ancestor, Tan Gong.

Bronze ritual vessels in the Shang artistic tradition also continued to be made by Zhou artisans. Over time, a distinct Zhou style emerged that employed different motifs and decorations as well as unusual forms. While some Zhou bronzes were expertly done, the quality declined in later

years, possibly because iron had been introduced and many artisans turned their attention to the production of iron weapons and implements. "Chariots, swords and the firing mechanism for crossbows formed the staple ingredients of the arms race," write historians Yong Yap and Arthur Cotterell, "so that princes and the great noble families vied with each other to attract the best technicians of the day."[37]

LITERATURE OF THE EARLY ZHOU

Creativity among the Zhou was not limited to bronze casting, but was also manifested in music and literature, for which a foundation had already been laid. For example, Emperor Shun of the Xia dynasty is said to have appointed a minister of music to serve in his government. A well-developed system of writing was already present during the Shang dynasty, and it is likely that the Shang had developed a body of literature that was lost during the rebellion. By the Early Zhou period, then, the cultural environment was already favorable for the creation of musical and literary works. The duke of Zhou himself was reportedly an accomplished musician and composer of poetry and songs.

It is from the Zhou dynasty that one of the oldest literary works comes. An ancient Chinese literary classic compiled and published during the Zhou dynasty is the *Book of Songs*, an anthology of Chinese verse. It consists of a collection of 305 poems from various sources and different time periods. "They are rhymed,"

Blunden and Elvin report, "with a ballad-like terseness, and always controlled and rational in mood. All of them were set to tunes—love songs, laments, satires, encomia [praises], work chanteys, and odes for feasting, worship and hunting."[38] Songs in the collection were performed on special occasions at the royal court. Singing was accompanied by instrumental music and expressive dancing to enhance the pomp and pageantry important in the lives of royalty.

The *Book of Songs* was very popular in its day, and its appearance during the Early Zhou seems to indicate a desire on the part of Zhou scholars to preserve important aspects of Chinese culture. To modern scholars, the *Book of Songs* is an invaluable source of information about the lives of everyday people in ancient China, which the bronzes, oracle bones, and official records do not reveal.

Another literary work that appeared during the Early Zhou dynasty, the *Book of Change,* or in Chinese, *Yijing* or *I Ching,* had as its theme the ancient practice of divining the future. A significant decrease in the number of oracle bones and shells in Western Zhou archaeological sites at first led scholars to assume that by the time of the Zhou divining was becoming less important.

However, an alternate explanation is that another method of divination, requiring only a handful of plant stalks, was replacing oracle bones and tortoise shells. This method had been handed down orally for centuries, but sometime in the Early Zhou dynasty, it was codified and published.

"This form of divination," writes historian Milton W. Meyer, "involved the shuffling and drawing of even or odd number of stalks, usually of milfoil, a common herb, to form short or long lines of a trigram [three-line figure]."[39] The trigrams were mathematically combined into sixty-four hexagrams (six-line figures), whose mystical meanings were explained in the *I Ching.*

The *I Ching* became a classic in ancient times and remains so today, twenty-five centuries later. The *I Ching* divining method gradually developed into a complex philosophy of decision making in life rather than a simple predictor of rain on a certain day or a successful hunt. History professor David N. Keightley explains:

> Where the Shang turned to bone cracks to consult the ancestral spirits or other powers about particular problems of government and personal life, the Zhou increasingly used the hexagrams to stimulate reflections upon the nature of life and action in general. . . . The *Yijing* was beloved of Confucius—who is said to have worn his own copy out—and it continued to be consulted by Chinese statesmen right down to the nineteenth century.[40]

END OF THE WESTERN ZHOU

While art and literature were beginning to flower within the Zhou dynasty, Zhou kings were finding it increasingly difficult to maintain control over the widespread empire. Their military superiority was

A Chinese Literary Classic

Scholars believe that oracle bone divining gradually gave way to another ancient method that was not recorded in book form until the Early Zhou dynasty. The method is best known in the Western world as I Ching (Yijing *in pinyin, or the* Book of Change *in English). Originally a simple method of divining,* I Ching *gradually took on deeper mystical uses and meanings. In the following excerpt from* The Taoist I Ching, *translator Thomas Cleary recounts its origins and development.*

I Ching, the "Book of Change," is considered the oldest of the Chinese classics, and has throughout its history commanded unsurpassed prestige and popularity. Containing several layers of text and given numerous levels of interpretation, it has captured continuous attention for well over two thousand years. It has been considered a book of fundamental principles by philosophers, politicians, mystics, alchemists, yogins, diviners, sorcerers, and more recently by scientists and mathematicians.

Traditionally, the *I Ching* is attributed to four authors: Fu Hsi, a prehistoric chieftain of perhaps c. 3000 B.C.E.; King Wen, an eleventh-century B.C.E. leader; the Duke of Chou [Zhou], son of King Wen; and Confucius, humanistic philosopher of the sixth to fifth centuries B.C. All of these names represent outstanding figures in the birth and development of Chinese civilization. Fu Hsi is a cultural prototype believed to have taught his people the arts of hunting, fishing, and animal husbandry; he is credited with the invention of the sixty-four signs on which the *I Ching* is based. King Wen and the Duke of Chou, founders of the great Chinese Chou Dynasty, are held up to history as models of enlightened rule; they are said to have collected or composed sayings attached to the sixty-four signs and to each of the six lines of which every sign is constructed. Confucius was an outstanding scholar and educator, known as an early transmitter of the Chinese classics and credited with commentaries that eventually became incorporated into the body of the *I Ching.* In recent times, however, these commentaries are commonly ascribed not to Confucius himself but to anonymous representatives of the school of thought he is said to have founded.

Precisely what lore, secret or open, was attached to the original signs of the *I Ching* in remote antiquity is a mystery and a matter of speculation. Fu Hsi lived before the development of writing as it is now known in China, and according to one belief he invented the *I Ching* signs as a system of notation, replacing a yet more ancient and cruder system.

being challenged by barbarians who had acquired bronze weapons themselves and had learned to build fortified cities.

Internal problems were mounting also. As the lords of the feudal provinces grew richer and more independent, they began neglecting or ignoring their responsibilities to the royal clan. "Eventually the feudal dukes of the various states grew too powerful," author Robert Silverberg declares, "and the center failed to hold."[41]

In 771 B.C., the center collapsed when a coalition of discontented lords and nomadic tribesmen staged an uprising against the Zhou ruler, King You. According to one story of his downfall, King You seems to have lacked the integrity of his illustrious predecessors. Morton reports, "In 771, the Zhou king suffered a severe defeat by a nomad tribe. . . . It is said that the monarch had previously had the alarm beacons lit for raising the levy of troops simply in order to see his favorite concubine laugh, for she was a petulant lady. When the real attack came, the soldiers disregarded the beacon fires and refused to muster."[42]

Caught unprotected, King You was assassinated by the rebels. Having no wish to bring down the dynasty, however, the rebels placed one of the king's sons on the throne as a puppet ruler. The rebellious princes then went back to their respective domains and conducted their own governments and waged their own private wars almost as if there were no dynastic system.

Afraid for his safety, the new king moved his capital eastward to Luoyang, where he and his successors survived for centuries as powerless figureheads. "The [Zhou] kings gradually lost their power and authority," Yap and Cotterell comment, "retaining undisputed only a religious function in the small and impoverished royal domain surrounding Luoyang."[43] Because that religious function included appeasement of powerful ancestors, even princes openly hostile to Zhou emperors allowed them to survive. Aside from their religious duties, however, emperors of the Late Zhou period exerted little or no influence on politics.

Historians mark these events as the beginning of the Eastern or Late Zhou dynasty, an era of contradictions in which unceasing conflict was accompanied by great strides in philosophy, art, and literature.

4 The Eastern (Late) Zhou: Conflict and Creativity

When the rebellion was staged against the Zhou king in 771 B.C., the fragmentation of the Zhou empire was already well underway. "At the beginning of the Eastern Zhou period," writes historian Stephen Haw, "there were some 170 states. Most were small, but a few, especially around the borders of the Chinese culture area, where there was room to expand at the expense of the barbarians, were large."[44]

The large states numbered around a dozen, and as the power of the Zhou kings ebbed, these aggressive kingdoms began to swallow up smaller ones. Not only their territories but also their ambitions grew, so that when all the weaker states had been overrun, the large states turned against one another. The Eastern Zhou period, then, is characterized by constant warfare, which became more and more lethal with the gradual introduction of new weapons and new military strategies.

Historians traditionally divide the Eastern Zhou dynasty into two parts, the Spring and Autumn period (770–481 B.C.) and the Warring States period (403–221 B.C.). The names are taken from the titles of two books written by early Chinese chroniclers about the periods, *Spring and Autumn Annals* and *The Strategies of the Warring States.* Authorship of the former work has been attributed to Confucius, but many scholars doubt the claim. The Warring States volume is a collection of documents and stories by unknown authors. There is no specific historical event that separates the periods. Rather, the two are distinguished by the scale and intensity of the conflicts that took place among the lords of the domains and by the cultural changes that resulted from all-out warfare.

SPRING AND AUTUMN PERIOD

In the Spring and Autumn period, the lords of the various states still gave lip service to the Zhou kings in their capital city at Luoyang. Though the kings no longer had control over the day-to-day affairs of the kingdom, a compelling religious connection between lord and king could not be ignored. Haw explains:

> Although the king had no real power over the lords of the states, they could not treat him as what he had actually become: the ruler of nothing more than a small and weak state, much

less powerful than many of his supposed subordinates. To do so would have challenged the whole basis of their own authority, for if the king had no divine authority to rule, then nor had they. The strength of the old ideas was such that it took centuries for them to change.[45]

Under the pretense of honoring the king, the lords went about the business of running their kingdoms and fighting one another.

WARFARE IN THE SPRING AND AUTUMN PERIOD

Warfare in the Spring and Autumn period was very much like that of the preceding Zhou period—attacks on enemy settlements by chariot and cavalry units armed with bronze weapons, backed up by peasant foot soldiers armed with Neolithic weapons.

This was the age of chivalrous war, when a rigid but polite set of combat rules was observed by both sides, often with

During the Spring and Autumn period of the Eastern Zhou dynasty, chariot and cavalry units used bronze weapons such as these dagger axes.

much pomp and pageantry. Describing this type of warfare, historian Jacques Gernet writes:

> In remote antiquity and in the [Spring and Autumn] age war was an aristocratic activity. The possession of chariots, horses, and weapons of bronze was restricted to the small number of men who took part in the battles, tournaments in the open countryside which tested the valor of the conflicting noble houses. The infantry, composed of peasants, played only a secondary part.[46]

The effect of such chivalrous customs is illustrated in the story of the Battle of Hong River, which took place in 638 B.C. between the states of Chu and Song. During the campaign, the duke of Song surprised the Chu troops while they were crossing a river. With such an advantage, he easily could have destroyed them. However, in the chivalrous manner of the times, he waited until all the Chu units had crossed the river and were arranged in battle formation before giving the signal to attack. The Chu forces responded to his gentlemanly behavior by crushing the Song army and disgracing the duke.

The duke did survive the battle; when he was asked why he failed to attack while he had the advantage, he replied, "The sage does not crush the feeble, nor give the order for the attack until the enemy have formed their ranks."[47]

Unfortunately, in the long run chivalry failed to save thousands from death in battle or the country from devastation by continuous wars. An era of complete anarchy was prevented only by the occasional emergence of an outstanding leader capable of bringing about a hegemony (coalition of states), usually in order to confront some greater threat.

One such leader was Duke Huan of the state of Qi. In order to repel the attacks of hostile nomadic tribes, he managed to unite several states under his leadership. During his forty-two-year tenure as hegemon (leader of the coalition), he served capably as both a diplomat and a military commander. He continued to pay homage and tribute to the Zhou king and even forced the Chu state to do the same. He may even have had dreams of uniting the country, but, according to the authors of *China's Buried Kingdoms,*

> it was a dream caught short by his death, after which the state of Qi failed to maintain its domination, and the struggle for the leadership role took on new energy. By the fifth century BC, the major states would abandon much of the pretense of obeisance to a central authority and fight for supremacy among themselves, without a single bow to the Zhou king.[48]

Although other hegemonies arose besides that of Duke Huan, none lasted long. From the fifth century B.C. throughout the next two centuries, total war prevailed among the surviving kingdoms, taking an appalling toll of human life and eventually transforming Chinese society from a collection of feudalistic states to a unified empire controlled from a strong central base.

CHIVALROUS WARRIORS

In early Chinese dynasties, wars were often contests between aristocratic lords who followed a strict set of chivalrous combat rules. The following excerpt from China: A Cultural History *by Arthur Cotterell tells a true story of battle chivalry that occurred between warriors of the states of Chu and Qin.*

Before the battle of Pi in 595 BC three Chu heroes taunted the Jin lines: one drove the chariot, the second loosed arrows, and the third protected the horses from foot-soldiers with a long spear. Pursued by a squadron of Jin charioteers, the Chu adventurers were making a daring escape, when a stag leaped up before them and they downed it with their last arrow. As a consequence of this, they halted and presented the beast to their pursuers, who accepted the gift and broke off the chase. In letting the Chu chariot get away the Jin nobles admitted the prowess and politeness of their foe.

THE WARRING STATES PERIOD

At the beginning of the Warring States period, only eight or nine independent states remained. It was becoming clear that nothing short of complete victory by one of them would stop the fighting. In earlier days, conflicts had been sporadic and relatively brief, but in the Warring States period, this more limited type of warfare gave way to prolonged battles and lengthy sieges of enemy cities. The objectives of war had changed as well. In former times, Haw reports, "The object of attacks was normally to seize a part or whole of the territory of the state attacked, or to force it to adhere to a particular alliance."[49] In the Warring States period, however, the goal became complete domination or even annihilation of the enemy.

Not just the purpose but the making of war changed. War making became a profession all its own. Commanders and officers of armies were no longer chosen solely because of their aristocratic backgrounds, but for their skill in the art of war. War making changed in other ways as well. The role of chariots, which had been crucial in early Chinese warfare, was much diminished as battles more frequently occurred in places where they could not operate effectively. Because charioteers came mainly from the noble classes, this new style of warfare further diminished the role of aristocrats in war. For the first time, the despised foot soldier gained prestige.

Whereas foot soldiers had played only a minor role in traditional skirmishes of earlier times, massive battles and drawn-out sieges now demanded extensive use of infantry. Those who formerly had no hope of improving their status in the rigid class system of ancient China found themselves in positions of authority gained through special martial skills or outstanding bravery displayed in battle. The number of heads a warrior took in battle counted for more than his lineage when promotions were handed out.

War became so pervasive that the military establishment emerged as the dominant social institution during the Warring States period. Princes were forced to increase the size of their armies, both to defend against attack and to move offensively against other kingdoms. Consequently, a major portion of a state's energy and resources were diverted to waging war.

For example, iron technology was encouraged in the quest for better weapons. Priority was given to the construction of highways and bridges, and to the improvement of transportation for moving armies and equipment. Projects to increase agricultural production, including flood control and irrigation, were escalated in order to feed the troops.

While all of these developments benefited domestic life as well, their major purpose was to build up a formidable fighting force in an era when weakness meant subjugation. Of all the wartime innovations, however, new weapons in the hands of enlarged infantry units most dramatically changed the character of Chinese warfare.

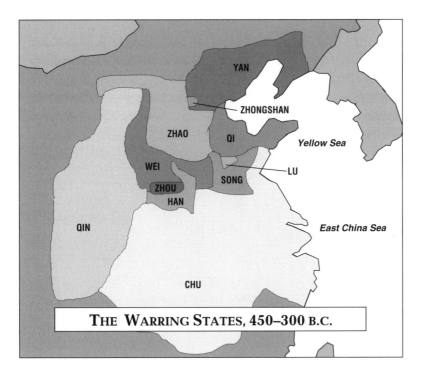

THE WARRING STATES, 450–300 B.C.

With the development of new types of warfare, chariots, some with richly gilded appendages like these bronze fittings, all but vanished from the battlefield.

THE NEW WEAPONS

Although bronze swords had been used by nobility in the Early Zhou period, swords did not come into widespread use until the Warring States period, when iron-smelting technology made it possible to produce them more cheaply and in quantity. Archaeologists have excavated ironworks dating to the fourth or fifth century B.C. However, the advanced design and craftsmanship of iron utensils dating to this period suggest that iron technology had developed much earlier.

In the fifth century B.C., an even more formidable weapon than the iron sword appeared: the crossbow, which was much more accurate, fast, and deadly than traditional bows. It was especially valued for its use by peasant infantry. Over the next hundred years, this invention revolutionized warfare. "By 300 BC," historian Patricia Buckley Ebrey writes, "states were sending out armies of hundreds of thousands of drafted foot-soldiers, often accompanied by mounted warriors. When armed with the powerful newly introduced crossbow, farmers could be made into effective soldiers, able to shoot further than horsemen carrying light bows."[50]

While a certain amount of skill and training was needed for operating a crossbow, it did not require the same techniques as a traditional bow held in one hand and stretched with the other. A crossbow was stretched and cocked with the archer's foot and the arrows were released by a trigger mechanism. "With levers arranged in three moving parts, it could hold a heavy-tension load yet be easily and smoothly released,"[51] explains historian W. Scott Morton. Easily aimed, crossbows made even the rawest peasant recruit a potentially deadly opponent.

In addition to decimating enemy troops, crossbows were used to disable chariots by propelling shafts into the moving wheels. Tactics such as these, which would have been impermissible in chivalrous fighting, became part of a new kind of calculated warfare whose object was to win by any possible means.

New Tactics

Historians estimate the states of Chu and Qin each could field over a million troops during the Warring States period. Obviously, armies of this size were a major investment, which had to be protected by careful military strategy and shrewd battle tactics. In fact, the oldest known book on the art of warfare comes from this period.

Entitled *The Art of War,* it was written by a well-known philosopher and teacher of the time, Sun Zi. Ebrey reports that in his book Sun Zi "not only discussed battle tactics but also the gathering of intelligence and other ways to deceive the enemy and win wars without combat."[52]

Most of the time, however, the destinies of states were decided by armies in the field. Increasingly, warfare meant laying

As with preceding dynasties, during the Eastern Zhou possession of objects like this jade sword sheath was reserved for aristocrats.

siege to cities protected by enormous walls of rammed earth. Sieges sometimes went on for months until the inhabitants were starved out or the walls were breached by the attackers. The new warfare took an enormous toll of human life, as compassion and mercy had no place in Late Zhou battle tactics. Captives taken in battle were slaughtered on the spot in great numbers.

Discipline within armies was also severe. Just how severe is related in *The Art of War* by Sun Zi:

> The Military Law states: 'Those who when they should advance do not do so and those who when they should retire do not do so are beheaded.' When Wu Ch'i fought against Ch'in [Qin], there was an officer who before battle was joined was unable to control his ardour. He advanced and took a pair of heads and returned. Wu Ch'i ordered him beheaded.
>
> The Army Commissioner admonished him, saying, 'This is a talented officer; you should not behead him.' Wu Ch'i replied, 'I am confident he is an officer of talent, but he is disobedient.' Thereupon he beheaded him.[53]

Social and cultural transformations brought about by centuries of warfare, particularly those allowing peasant soldiers to improve their social status, brought tremendous pressure to bear on the Zhou feudalistic system of lords and vassals, and eventually dismantled it altogether.

SOCIAL AND CULTURAL CHANGES

During the relatively stable Western Zhou period, the feudal system had worked fairly well. It began to decline in Eastern Zhou times, and by the Warring States period, it was all but gone. "The process of absorption of small states by more powerful ones led to the downfall of many noble families," Haw reports. "Rulers of conquered states might, if they were lucky, be allowed to remain in their old territory as subordinates of their conquerors. At worst, they might be reduced to the status of slaves. Their fate was usually shared by their ministers and retainers."[54] The end result was the concentration of power in the hands of only a few powerful men. With such a concentration the old feudal system broke down.

The fall of feudalism also disrupted the lives of thousands of peasants and farmers who had received some measure of security working the lands of aristocratic lords. Set adrift when their lords were vanquished, many sought employment in commercial enterprises in the cities. As a result, the village life on which many people depended was badly disrupted.

SCHOOLS OF THOUGHT

Bitter wars and social upheaval led many thinkers to ponder the nature of human society. Beginning in the late Spring and Autumn period and extending through the Warring States period, a succession of brilliant political and social philosophers appeared whose works are still read and pondered today.

At first, it seems paradoxical that creative works could have come out of the terror and violence of the Late Zhou period. But amid a crumbling social order, it was natural that some scholars would turn their thoughts to what constitutes a perfect state and how to bring it about. Moreover, not all kings and lords were tyrannical and brutal. In fact, many of them encouraged scholarly and artistic activities. Even kings who were not particularly interested in intellectual pursuits themselves were constantly on the lookout for assistants and officials who could help them defend their territories or conquer those of others.

Due to this encouragement of intellectual activity, the Late Zhou period became known not only for its wars, but for the richness and diversity of its thinkers. So many ideas were set forth that the term "One Hundred Schools of Thought" has been applied to the period. Itinerant teachers would go about the countryside sharing their ideas with whoever would listen and trying to attract pupils. Although many of these philosophies died along with the teachers who promoted them, several had lasting consequences for China and indeed for the world.

THE PHILOSOPHY OF CONFUCIUS

Probably the best-known of these teachers was a scholar known as Kung Fu Zi (Confucius, as he is called in the Western world). Confucius was born around 551 B.C. in the small state of Lu in eastern China. Reliable data about his family background is scarce. He might have had aristocratic ancestors, but the family into which he was born was not wealthy and he held no hereditary rank.

Professor H. G. Creel says of him, "He had to make his own living, at tasks that were more or less menial. He was able to study, but seems to have been largely self-taught. These experiences undoubtedly gave him a close view of the sufferings of the common people about which he became deeply concerned."[55]

Confucius's outspoken concern for the common people often put him at odds with those in the seats of power. For instance, when an influential lord (who embodied all of the ruthless characteristics Confucius despised) asked him how to deal with thieves in his domain, Confucius answered, "If you, sir, did not covet things that don't belong to you, they wouldn't steal if you paid them to."[56]

Although he sought change, Confucius was not a rebel who wanted to violently overthrow the old order. His goal was to improve the system from within by training students for government positions where they might serve as examples of fairness and honesty. Confucius himself actively sought a high government post where his ideas would have a better chance of being heard, but it was never offered to him.

Confucius's teachings were social, not religious. He never claimed to be divine or have a monopoly on truth. Neither did he leave any writings. After his death,

The teachings of Confucius had a monumental impact on Chinese political and social thinking.

however, some of his pupils collected his sayings and published them in a book called *Analects*. Many of his pupils became famous in their own right and added their own personal variations to his teachings. In later centuries, a kind of cult worship grew up around him, attributing many ideas and sayings to him that probably were not his own, even some with which he would have disagreed.

Nevertheless, from the *Analects*, the fundamentals of Confucius's philosophy may be discerned. His goal was the establishment of a just and orderly society

THE *ANALECTS* OF CONFUCIUS

China's most enduring and well loved teacher, Confucius, lived in the Late Zhou period. Confucius did not write books, but his pupils gathered many of his sayings into a text called the Analects. *The following selections from the* Analects *are excerpted from* Sources of Chinese Tradition, *vol. 1, edited by William Theodore de Bary. (Numbers indicate the sections from which the quotations came.)*

The Master said: "Lead the people by laws and regulate them by penalties, and the people will try to keep out of jail, but will have no sense of shame. Lead the people by virtue and restrain them by the rules of decorum, and the people will have a sense of shame, and moreover will become good." [II: 3]

Confucius said: "Riches and honor are what every man desires, but if they cannot be obtained only by transgressing the right way, they must not be held. Poverty and lowliness are what every man detests, but if they can be avoided only by transgressing the right way, they must not be evaded. If a gentleman departs from humanity, how can he bear the name?" [IV: 5]

Tzu Kung [a follower] asked about the gentleman. Confucius said: "The gentleman first practices what he preaches and then preaches what he practices." [II: 13] . . . "The gentleman is always calm and at ease; the inferior man is always worried and full of distress." [VII: 36] . . . "The gentleman cherishes virtue; the inferior man cherishes possessions." [IV: 11] . . . "The gentleman makes demands on himself; the inferior man makes demands on others." [XV: 20] . . . "The gentleman seeks to enable people to succeed in what is good but does not help them in what is evil. The inferior man does the contrary." [XII: 16]

Confucius said: "By nature men are pretty much alike; it is learning and practice that set them apart." [XVII: 2]

Confucius said: "In education there are no class distinctions." [XV: 38]

Confucius said: "Yu [*his student*], shall I teach you what knowledge is? When you know a thing, say that you know it; when you do not know a thing, admit that you do not know it. That is knowledge." [II: 17]

Tzu Kung [a follower] asked: "Is there any one word that can serve as a principle for the conduct of life?" Confucius said: "Perhaps the word 'reciprocity': Do not do to others what you would not want others to do to you." [XV: 23]

by means of well-defined reciprocal roles: ruler to subject, husband to wife, parent to child, and so on. To maintain order, Confucius believed, one role in each reciprocal set had to be dominant over the other, which to Confucius meant rulers over subjects, husbands over wives, and parents over children. Fundamental to these relationships, however, was the assumption that the dominant member would treat the subordinate member with benevolence and fairness. In turn, the subordinate member's duty was to reciprocate with obedience and loyalty.

Underlying the entire system, and vital to its success, was the integrity of political rulers. Historians Yong Yap and Arthur Cotterell comment, "[Confucius's] this-worldly doctrine was a feudal ethic, which expected the prince to rule with benevolence and sincerity, avoiding the use of force at all costs. Like the Duke of Zhou and other great rulers of the past, he had to manage affairs so that justice was enjoyed by every subject."[57]

Since there were few takers for such noble ideas in Late Zhou times, Confucius's system was never wholly adopted by the Zhou dynasty or any other. Nevertheless, his prescription for empathetic human relationships profoundly influenced Chinese political and social thinking from his own day to the present. In addition to his teachings, another of Confucius's lasting contributions was the compilation and preservation of ancient Chinese literary classics, many of which have survived to the present day.

The adulation heaped upon Confucius after his death would have come as a great surprise to him. When he died in 479 B.C., he felt that his life had been a failure. "Yet few human lives have influenced history more profoundly than that of Confucius," writes Creel. "If we look for the secret of his appeal, it seems probable that it lies in his insistence on the supremacy of human values."[58]

THE PHILOSOPHY OF DAOISM

A school of thought very different from that of Confucius also gained popularity in Late Zhou times. Called Daoism, its origins are clouded in mystery. Unlike the straightforward maxims of Confucius, Daoist philosophy is mystical and difficult to comprehend. Dao, which means "the way," is defined by Ebrey as "the indivisible, indescribable, immaterial force or energy that is the source of all that exists or happens."[59]

Daoists identified with this force and sought to understand their place in the great scheme of nature. Daoist teachers urged their followers to surrender themselves to the cosmic current. Their slogan was *wu-wei*, do nothing. This did not necessarily mean sitting motionless (although some Daoists did that, too), but being indifferent to social pressures. Happiness lay in ceasing to strive for wealth, power, and social position.

In matters of government, Daoists held an opposite view from that of Confucius. Whereas Confucius wanted good people to be involved in government to make it better, Daoists retreated from it, respecting the natural law of the cosmos rather than

THE WISDOM OF ANCIENT DAOIST PHILOSOPHERS

The following two excerpts are scriptures from an ancient book called Laozi (Classic of the Way and Its Power). Laozi *sets forth the principles of Daoism, a mystical philosophy that became prominent in the Warring States period. Daoists advised individuals to avoid worldly ambitions and counseled rulers to govern lightly. The first selection is excerpted from* Chinese Thought: From Confucius to Mao Tse-Tung *by H. G. Creel. The second is taken from* The World's Great Scriptures *by Lewis Browne.*

If you would not spill the wine,
Do not fill the glass too full.
If you wish your blade to hold its edge,
Do not try to make it over-keen.
If you do not want your house to be
molested by robbers,
Do not fill it with gold and jade.
Wealth, rank, and arrogance add up to ruin,
As surely as two and two are four.
When you have done your work
and established your fame, withdraw!
Such is the way of Heaven.

* * * * *

The Art of Government

The more prohibitions there are,
the poorer the people become.
The more sharp weapons there are,
The more prevailing chaos there is in the state.
The more skills of technique,
The more cunning things are produced.
The greater the number of statues,
The greater the number of thieves and brigands.
Therefore the Sage says:
I do nothing and the people are
reformed of themselves.
I love quietude and the people
are righteous of themselves.
I deal in no business and the people
grow rich by themselves.
I have no desires and the people are
simple and honest by themselves.

human authority. If there had to be governments, the Daoists believed, then the best ones were those that governed least.

Many Daoists became recluses, living apart from society. For those who could not do that, Daoism offered a psychological escape from the rigid social constraints that controlled their everyday lives. Forced to be Confucianists in their daily lives, they could still be Daoists in private moments. The popularity of Daoism in the Late Zhou period also sprang from the despair and hopelessness experienced by many people in that war-torn era. Professor Eva Wong explains:

> During those times, China was in a state of political and social chaos. . . . The strong survived and the weak perished. . . . Politics were dirty. Family members spied on each other and assassinations were common. Treachery and intrigue were widespread among government officials. One could certainly lose one's life by playing the dangerous game of politics, but being virtuous and loyal did not guarantee safety. Under these circumstances, what could people do?[60]

What many people did during the Warring States period, Wong suggests, was seek comfort in Daoist ideals of inner serenity and selflessness. Moreover, Daoism's appeal did not end with the Warring States period, nor has it been confined to China. Today, twenty-five centuries after its inception, Daoism endures in many other nations around the world, becoming particularly dynamic in times of social upheaval.

LEGALISM

Although Confucianism and Daoism differed in many respects, they both sought to defend common people against despotic rulers. An opposing viewpoint called Legalism, which began to gain ground in the Warring States period, defended the autocratic behavior of rulers as right and necessary. Legalism took the view that human beings are basically evil and must be restrained for their own good.

Han Feizi, one of the leading proponents of Legalism during the Warring States period, defends this point of view:

> When the sage rules the state, he does not count on people doing good of themselves, but employs such measures as will keep them from doing any evil. If he counts on people doing good of themselves, there will not be enough such people to be numbered by the tens in the whole country. But if he employs such measures as will keep them from doing evil, then the entire state can be brought up to a uniform standard. Inasmuch as the administrator has to consider the many but disregard the few, he does not busy himself with morals, but with laws.[61]

Many rulers seized upon Legalist philosophy as a justification for severe punishments, heavy taxation, and enforced labor of the common people. Toward the end of the Warring States period, the stern measures of Legalism became more than theory and were put into practice in the state of Qin. Under strict laws and harsh

Music for a Wealthy Zhou Ruler

Not all pleasures and entertainments ceased during the prolonged warfare of the Late Zhou era, particularly among the wealthy. In 1978 many types of musical instruments were found in the excavation of a nobleman's tomb. The most spectacular was a large set of bells cast in bronze. Patricia Buckley Ebrey describes this unusual find in the Cambridge Illustrated History of China.

Archaeologists have unearthed quite a few sets of instruments used in court performances in Zhou times. Key instruments were stone chimes, bronze drums, stringed lute-like instruments, bamboo flutes, and sets of bells. The biggest cache of instruments was discovered in the tomb (c. 433 BC) of Marquis Yi of Zeng, ruler of a petty state in modern Hubei just north of the great state of Chu. In the tomb were 124 instruments, including drums, flutes, mouth organs, pan pipes, zithers, a 32-chime lithophone [stone chimes], and a 64-piece bell set. The zithers have from five to twenty-five strings and vary in details of their construction; they may have come from different regions and been used for performances of regional music. The bells bear inscriptions that indicate their pitches and reveal that they were gifts from the king of Chu. The precision with which the bells were cast indicates that the art of bell-making had reached a very advanced state.

This sixty-four piece set of bells, discovered in the tomb of Marquis Yi, was a gift from the king of Chu.

punishments, its people were obedient, and its armies were well trained and feared far and wide for their bravery and discipline in battle.

The End of the Zhou Dynasty

Beginning around 314 B.C., the Qin armies began overrunning and annexing vast areas of neighboring states. In 256, Qin annexed the by then tiny state of Zhou, officially bringing an end to the beleaguered Zhou dynasty. In 247, King Zheng came to the throne, where he was surrounded by ministers who promoted the theory of Legalism.

During the next ten years, King Zheng's armies defeated all the remaining independent states in China one by one. The last, the state of Qi, fell in 221 B.C., when King Zheng was still a very young man. He had done what no other leader before him had been able to do, unite all the states of China under one central government. His own state of Qin was now supreme.

5 The Qin Dynasty: Unification and Imperialism

The state of Qin, which lay to the west of the state of Zhou, was looked upon as semibarbarian by people of the more cultured states to the east. Its responsibility was to raise horses and defend the Zhou from nomadic tribes along its borders. After the Zhou kings lost control, Qin leaders began to make sweeping changes in the political and social structure of their state, causing it to rise steadily in wealth, power, and military might.

The first of these strong leaders was Lord Shang. A proponent of Legalism, Lord Shang came from the state of Wei to be an adviser to Duke Xiao, ruler of Qin. Around 360 B.C. he initiated a series of drastic reforms that were designed to break the political power held by aristocratic families. With their vast landholdings and inherited privileges, wealthy clans had virtually become separate domains within the Qin state. Lord Shang's goal was to bring them firmly under the authority of the Qin ruler, in order to make the central government stronger and more efficient.

REFORMS OF LORD SHANG

Certain conditions prevailing in the state of Qin made this transformation somewhat easier. For instance, in the vast Qin domain, countless acres of unproductive land were left unclaimed by wealthy families. The state began to reclaim this land, which government officials used for the betterment of the kingdom. Peasants and farmers working the reclaimed lands were no longer under the control of feudal lords, and the taxes they paid went to the state.

Growing commercialism also helped change the base of power. Historian Jacques Gernet explains:

> Whereas in the [Spring and Autumn] age, commerce remained confined to luxury products such as pearls and jade and was the province of merchants who had special relations with princely courts, the following age saw the development of a considerable trade in ordinary consumer goods (cloth, cereals, salt), and in metals,

wood, leather, and hides. . . . These new activities lay outside the traditional framework of the palace economy with its bodies of craftsmen controlled by palace nobles: potters, cartwrights, bow-makers, curriers, basket-makers, builders, and so on.[62]

A new economic class, the merchants, arose to trade in these goods. Great amounts of money that were taxable by the central government were thus generated by the merchant class. The rise of commercialism also created a new class of workers, freeing them from dependence on the nobility. Peasants were no longer forced to work as serfs and were even allowed to buy and sell land.

Lord Shang's reforms were not limited to breaking up the nobility, however. He also instituted a series of strict measures aimed at weakening the extended family system to make individuals more responsible to the central government. "Shang Yang passed a law that imposed a double tax on persons with two or more adult sons living with them," write historians Yong Yap and Arthur Cotterell. "Communal ownership gave place to individual possessions and nuclear families."[63]

Moreover, Lord Shang's laws were designed to terrify the people into submission. "The state organized all families into mutual responsibility groups," historian Patricia Buckley Ebrey reports, "making each person liable for any crime committed by any other member of their group. Ordinary residents also had heavy obligations to the state for taxes and labour service and could not travel without permits."[64]

Under Lord Shang's iron hand, the state of Qin grew rich and powerful, as did Lord Shang himself. His luck ran out, however, when his patron and protector, Duke Xiao, died. The succeeding ruler, who despised Lord Shang for past offenses, accused him of plotting a rebellion. When Lord Shang attempted to flee, he was slain, along with his entire family, much as he himself had advocated in his laws the punishment of the families of offenders as well as the offenders themselves.

In spite of universal hatred for him among their subjects, succeeding rulers recognized that Lord Shang's methods, though harsh, had created a very efficient central government. Therefore, with the help of other advisers every bit as cunning, subsequent Qin rulers carried on where Lord Shang left off.

FINAL VICTORY

For the next century, the rise of the state of Qin continued with the acquisition of more and more territory through military conquest. In 247 B.C., Prince Zheng ascended the throne. Because he was not yet of age, he was served by two prime ministers, Lu Buwei and Li Si. Nine years later, when Zheng came of age, he launched the final drive to subdue the remaining independent states. Historian Arthur Cotterell describes the final victories:

Although the Qin army suffered reverses at the hands of Zhao and Chu, superior manpower and resources

AN ATTEMPT TO ASSASSINATE KING ZHENG

While he was still King Zheng of Qin, an attempt was made on the life of the future First Emperor. The would-be killer, Jing Ke, purportedly came to present the king with the head of a renegade general who had been captured and executed, and to make him a gift of a map. In reality, he came to kill him with a poisoned dagger rolled up inside the map. Ancient historian Sima Qian records what happened next in this excerpt, quoted in China: A Cultural History *by Arthur Cotterell.*

King Zheng asked to see the map. Thereupon Jing Ke took out the map, unrolled it, and exposed the dagger. Seizing the sleeve of the Qin king with his left hand, Jing Ke grasped the dagger with the right and struck at him. In alarm King Zheng leapt backwards so that his sleeve tore off. Though he tried hard, the king was unable to draw his sword, which was very long. . . . Jing Ke pursued the Qin king who ran round a pillar. The astounded courtiers were simply paralysed.

In Qin law a courtier was forbidden to carry weapons. Moreover, the royal guard was not permitted to enter the audience chamber unless summoned. At this critical moment there was not time to call for the soldiers anyway. Thus Jing Ke chased King Zheng who tried to ward off the dagger blows with his two joined hands.

At this juncture the court physician, one Xia Wuzu, struck Jing Ke with his medicine bag. King Zheng, however, continued to dash round and round the pillar, so distraught was he. Then a courtier cried out: 'Put your sword behind you, king!' By so doing he found he could unsheath the weapon and wound Jing Ke in the left thigh. Disabled, Jing Ke raised his dagger and hurled it at the king, but it missed and hit a bronze pillar. King Zheng then wounded his assailant several more times. . . . Then it was that they killed Jing Ke. [As the only one who took action to save the king, the court physician was rewarded with a gift of gold.]

told in the end, Han going down in 230 BC, soon followed by Zhao (228 BC) and Wei (225 BC), but the decisive engagement did not occur till the year 223 BC when the rival state of Chu was vanquished. The over-running of Yan in 222 BC and the surrender of Qi without a fight a year later made the 'Tiger of Qin,' as Zheng was then called, the ruler of all China.[65]

To set himself above mere kings and princes of other states, the triumphant King Zheng took upon himself an exalted new name—Shi Huangdi. Shi means "first" and Huangdi literally means "august lord" or simply emperor. By choosing that name, the new king placed himself in distinguished company, as Huangdi had also been the name of the revered Yellow Emperor.

THE NEW ORDER

At the age of thirty-eight, Shi Huangdi set about transforming the whole of China from a loose confederation of feudal states controlled by competing aristocratic families into a powerful centralized state controlled by one supreme authority.

Shi Huangdi was a Legalist. The stern measures he introduced were regarded in Legalist theory as a means to an end, not the end itself. "The reforms were the expression of a mode of thinking which may be described as rational," Gernet states. "They aimed at substituting uniform rules for the multiplicity of rights, privileges, and customs which characterized the old society . . . with its aristocratic lines of descent, its bonds of dependence, and its hierarchies."[66]

Emperor Qin Shi Huangdi fought to unite all of China under his rule.

The First Emperor set about establishing the new order with great diligence. Although he was quite young when he came to power and was surrounded by older advisers, he was very much involved in the affairs of state, as Professor Ray Huang writes:

> The First Emperor traveled extensively, visiting not only the urban centers, but also the great mountains and rivers, the lakes and the high seas. He toured the capital city incognito at night. Although proud of his military exploits, Qin Shi-huang-di is not known to have ever commanded troops personally. On the other hand, he was a tireless worker. He set quotas for the amount of documents, by weight, that he must dispose of daily, not resting until his work was done.[67]

REORGANIZING THE EMPIRE

The major reforms Shi Huangdi put into place in the new Chinese empire may be summarized in three words—centralization, bureaucratization, and standardization.

Centralization was achieved by several means. First of all, ruling families from the conquered states were stripped of their titles and lands and forced to live near Xianyang, Shi Huangdi's capital city, near present day Xian. At Xianyang, they were closely watched by court officials for signs of disloyalty or rebelliousness. The empire was then divided into provinces (called commanderies) under the control of officers of the central government. To physically bind the empire together, road building and improvement in transportation methods were given high priority.

Armies of the former states were combined into one empirewide fighting force controlled by the royal court. Ownership of private arms was declared illegal and a mass surrender of weapons was ordered. Historian Derk Bodde writes, "Weapons were collected throughout the empire and brought to [Xianyang], where they were melted and cast into bells, bell supports, and twelve colossal human statues, each said to weigh nearly twenty-nine English tons . . . which were set up within the [Qin] palace enclosure."[68]

Hand in hand with centralization was bureaucratization, a system for organizing the work of administrative offices into clearly defined positions filled on the basis of merit rather than hereditary rank. In his quest for efficiency, Shi Huangdi brought talented people into the government, regardless of their status or place of origin. Careful business accounting was required of officeholders with rewards for diligence and stiff punishments for irresponsibility.

Bureaucratization also required the daily business of the empire to be conducted according to detailed rules and regulations. Bodde cites two examples from ancient records: "When a request is to be made about some matter, it must be done in writing. There can be no oral requesting, nor can it be entrusted [to a third person]. When documents are transmitted or received, the month, day and time of day of their sending and arrival must be recorded to expedite a reply."[69]

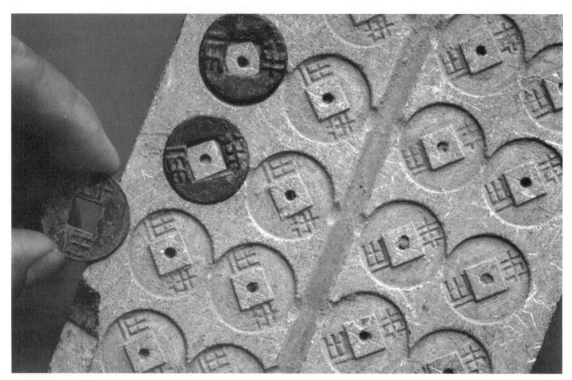

Qin Shi Huangdi standardized currency, making trade and tax collection easier.

STANDARDIZATION

Ruling a vast empire from a central location demanded that certain aspects of daily life be made uniform. The purpose of many standardization measures instituted under the Qin government was to facilitate trade and commerce within the empire. For example, under the Zhou dynasty, various items had been used as currency, including shells, gems, various types of coins, and other metal objects. All such money systems were replaced in the Qin dynasty with a common currency assigned a standard value. Round metal coins with holes in the center (so that they could be strung on a cord) were substi-

tuted throughout the empire. The new money system not only benefited trade, but made tax collection easier as well.

To further strengthen commercial activities, standardization was also required for weights and measurements and these laws were strictly enforced. Old records indicate that some of the enforced laborers on Shi Huangdi's building projects were those who had violated weight and measurement regulations.

An unusual standardization order was that all cart axles had to be the same length. "This may seem a strange requirement," historian Stephen Haw observes, "but in the conditions of the time it was eminently sensible. Roads were not well surfaced, and the wheels of the carts wore deep ruts in them. It was difficult, if not impossible, to haul carts over roads in which the ruts were not the same distance apart as the carts' wheels."[70]

The decree that inspired the greatest resistance, however, was the edict that Chinese writing should be standardized. Writing, which first appeared in the Shang dynasty, had remained relatively unchanged over the centuries. However, as the empire expanded and non-Chinese people were assimilated into it, regional variations had occurred.

Such variations caused problems in conducting the business of the empire. In a country where dozens of languages and dialects were spoken, the only universal form of communication was the written script. Shi Huangdi therefore decreed that a uniform set of written characters should be chosen and made the official script of the empire.

While the basic premise of this order was reasonable, the plan met with resistance from scholars who realized that much of the writings of the past would no longer be readable. Shi Huangdi was not moved by that argument, however, because he believed the present welfare of the state took precedence over past traditions. The script was therefore standardized, but scholars were able to translate some of the old writings into the new script in order to preserve them.

Ironically, it made no difference in the long run. In 213 B.C., after learning from his chief adviser, Li Si, that certain scholars were criticizing his reforms, Shi Huangdi (on Li Si's recommendation) ordered the burning of all books except a few on medicine, agriculture, and divination.

PERSONALITY OF THE EMPEROR

Outrageous acts such as burning the books made the First Emperor extremely unpopular. On two occasions the emperor narrowly survived assassination attempts. As a result, he gradually withdrew from public life into a closed circle

Acts like book burning and harsh punishments for violating the new weight and measurement laws made Qin Shi Huangdi extremely unpopular.

PRIME MINISTER LI SI RECOMMENDS BURNING THE BOOKS

To put an end to criticism of his rule from scholars, the First Emperor of China accepted a recommendation from Li Si, his chief minister, that all books (except certain ones enjoyed by the emperor) be burned. Li Si's recommendation is excerpted from Sources of Chinese Tradition, *edited by William Theodore de Bary.*

Memorial on the Burning of Books

In earlier times the empire disintegrated and fell into disorder, and no one was capable of unifying it. Thereupon the various feudal lords rose to power. In their discourses they all praised the past in order to disparage the present and embellished empty words to confuse the truth. Everyone cherished his own school of learning and criticized what had been instituted by the authorities. But at present Your Majesty possesses a unified empire . . . and has firmly established for yourself a position of sole supremacy. And yet these independent schools, joining with each other, criticize the codes of laws and instructions. . . . They seek a reputation by discrediting their sovereign; they appear superior by expressing contrary views, and they lead the lowly multitude in the spreading of slander. If such license is not prohibited, the sovereign power will decline above and partisan factions will form below. It would be well to prohibit this.

Your servant suggests that all the books in the imperial archives, save the memoirs of Ch'in, be burned. All persons in the empire, except members of the Academy of Learned Scholars, in possession of the *Book of Odes,* the *Book of History*, and discourses of the hundred philosophers should take them to the local governors and have them indiscriminately burned. Those who dare to talk to each other about the *Book of Odes* and the *Book of History* should be executed and their bodies exposed in the market place. Anyone referring to the past to criticize the present should, together with all members of his family, be put to death. Officials who fail to report cases that have come under their attention are equally guilty. After thirty days from the time of issuing the decree, those who have not destroyed their books are to be branded and sent to build the Great Wall. Books not to be destroyed will be those on medicine and pharmacy, divination by the tortoise and milfoil, and agriculture and arboriculture. People wishing to pursue learning should take the officials as their teachers.

of advisers and courtiers, thereby losing touch with the outside world.

Despite his isolation, Shi Huangdi managed to impose his will on his subjects. For example, Shi Huangdi was very superstitious, highly influenced by omens and dreams. This fact, along with his self-imposed isolation, caused him to become obsessed with a fear of dying. He thus began to search for a magic formula that would make him immortal. The hidden purpose of many of his travels was to consult oracles and magicians who might help him in his quest. At court, he retained a large group of sages whose job was to do the same. When they failed, he banished or executed them.

Stories of the emperor's cruelty abound. One possibly exaggerated account is that in a fit of rage, he ordered more than four hundred scholars buried alive for displeasing him by their criticisms and failure to find the eternal life formula. Often his anger erupted over personal affronts. Bodde describes such an incident:

> Once, looking from a mountaintop, the emperor was displeased to notice that the carriages and riders of the chancellor [Li Si] were very numerous. Someone told this to the chancellor, who diminished his entourage accordingly. The emperor, realizing that he had an informer, became angry. When nobody would admit guilt, he had all those who had been with him at the time arrested and executed.[71]

There is no doubt that Shi Huangdi was a despot in the strictest sense of the word, but later historians tried to present a more balanced appraisal of his reign. Historian W. Scott Morton says of him, "Qin Shi Huang Di, the First Emperor . . . was in many ways a ruthless tyrant. . . . But he laid down the main lines upon which the empire subsequently developed. In particular he produced a unified and centralized realm which remained the Chinese ideal for empire."[72]

IMPERIAL EXCESSES

Nevertheless, it is Shi Huangdi's well-documented excesses for which he is best known and which undoubtedly proved a main reason for his dynasty's short duration of only fifteen years. The construction of his own lavish tomb is a case in point. Work on it began even before he became emperor in the early days and continued until the time of his death at the age of forty-nine. Thousands of workers devoted their lives to the building of the tomb.

Traditional sources report that childless concubines of Shi Huangdi were sealed inside the tomb along with the emperor's body. Moreover, artisans and engineers who knew the secrets of the tomb's construction suffered the same fate. Although the tomb itself has not yet been excavated, Sima Qian wrote a description of it which appears in his book, *Records of the Historian*, published in the first century B.C.:

> As soon as the first emperor became king of Ch'in [in 246 B.C.] work was begun on his mausoleum at Mount

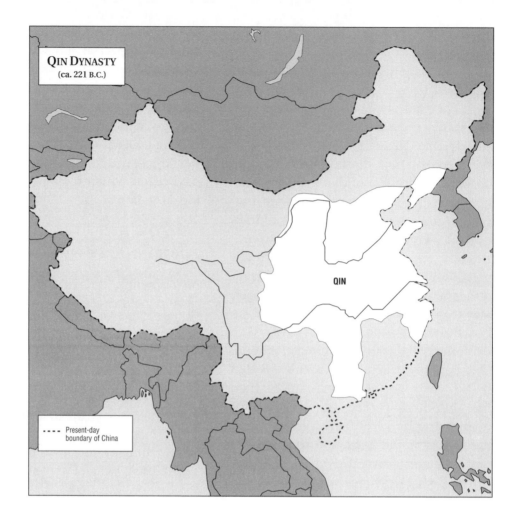

QIN DYNASTY
(ca. 221 B.C.)

QIN

- - - - Present-day
boundary of China

Li. After he won the empire [in 221 B.C.], more than 700,000 conscripts from all parts of China laboured there. They dug through three underground streams; they poured molten copper for the outer coffin; and they filled the burial chamber with models of palaces, towers and official buildings, as well as fine utensils, precious stones and rarities. Artisans were ordered to fix automatic crossbows so that grave robbers would be slain.

The waterways of the empire, the Yellow and Yang-tzu rivers, and even the great ocean itself, were represented by mercury and were made to flow mechanically. Above, the heavenly constellations were depicted, while below lay a representation of the earth. Lamps using whale oil were installed to burn for a long time.[73]

Whether Sima Qian's description is accurate remains to be seen. However, in

1974 an excavation near Shi Huangdi's burial mound revealed an unexpected find—an army of life-size terra-cotta (clay) figures, infantry, cavalry, and archery units in battle dress and formation. Terra-cotta charioteers and horses were also unearthed, along with imprints of wooden chariots, long since decayed. The clay army undoubtedly was designed to guard the emperor in the afterworld. After years of work at the site, archaeologists have uncovered only a small portion of Shi Huangdi's legacy. Preliminary investigations in other areas around the tomb indicate that many more exciting discoveries may lie below the surface.

Before his death, Shi Huangdi and his entourage lived in a grand manner. Dissatisfied with the palace in which he had resided as king, he commissioned an enormous and costly new one to be built near Xianyang, his capital city. In addition, many other grand palaces were built along the Wei River near Xianyang to which the leading families from conquered territories were moved after the Qin victory. According to early accounts, the palaces built for the transplanted families were replicas of the ones they left behind.

Near the tomb of Qin Shi Huangdi, an entire terra-cotta army was constructed to defend the emperor in the afterlife.

THE TERRA-COTTA ARMY OF QIN SHI HUANGDI

In 1974 farmers digging a well near the city of Xian in Shaanxi Province made an astonishing discovery—broken statues of ancient warriors modeled in terra-cotta. Upon further investigation, archaeologists uncovered an entire division of life-size clay soldiers buried about a half-mile from the gravesite of Shi Huangdi, First Emperor of China. In his book China: A Macro History, *author Ray Huang describes this silent army.*

The site is an enclosure of over three acres. It is estimated that no less than 7,000 life-size earthenware soldiers equipped with real weapons, real chariots, and pottery horses are protecting the resting place of their master. The entire scene is marked by its grand scale on the one hand and its dedication to details on the other. The figures of the soldiers seems to have been copied from live models; no two of them are alike. Their facial expression shows endless individuality. They all wear the same hairstyle; yet in each case there is a slight variation in the way the hair is combed, the whiskers are trimmed, and the braids are knotted. Their caps are decorated with patterned dots; their belts have metal hooks; their armor jackets are sculptured to indicate leather straps serving as fasteners; and their shoes have cleats on the soles. Their armor varies from that of the foot soldier to that of the cavalryman. . . . The poses of the earthenware statues are diverse; they are standing at attention, kneeling down to man crossbows, driving chariots, poised for hand-to-hand combat, each at the battle station called for by the overall tactics. In sum, what is represented is an entire division of Qin infantry, flanked by a formation of chariots and a squadron of cavalry, ready to go into combat at a moment's notice.

While the scale of this display is impressive, specialists speculate that more soldiers, horses, and chariots may be positioned on the southern flank of this division. Or, even more impressive, entire divisions of the same terra-cotta army may be deployed on the other three sides of the emperor's burial chamber, which would quadruple the scale of the present discovery.

The seven thousand terra-cotta statues seem to represent real people, for each one bears a different expression and no two are alike.

Like Shi Huangdi's tomb, the palaces were built by conscripted laborers, slaves, and convicts. Forced labor was also used to build an estimated 4,250 miles of roads throughout the empire. The construction of canals and massive earthen walls on the empire's borders were other projects on which thousands of unfortunate peasants were forced to devote their lives. Cotterell observes:

> Such extensive construction and engineering projects not only required huge amounts of manpower but also necessitated the assembly and transport of large quantities of building materials, thus imposing a heavy burden on the ordinary people. In the same way, the continual use of enforced labor throughout the empire had strained the allegiance of the peasantry, especially when it was maintained by the naked force of cruel punishments.[74]

THE DEATH OF SHI HUANGDI

None of Shi Huangdi's palaces or walled defenses could keep out what he feared most—his own death. Ironically, he died while on a trip seeking a potion for eternal life from certain Daoist magicians of whom he had heard. Accompanying him on the journey was Li Si, his minister; Zhao Gao, another high palace official; and Hu Hai, a favorite son (among the twenty sons he sired). Since no one except those three was allowed to see the emperor, they were able to pretend he was still alive, continuing to attend to him and consult with him in his carriage.

Traditional accounts tell that, being a long way from home, Shi Huangdi's body began to decay and give off an odor. To mask this, Li Si had a cart of salted fish placed in front of the emperor's carriage. If servants or other members of the entourage noticed anything unusual about this, they never said so, being terrified of the displeasure of the emperor and his ministers.

In this situation, it was not only the servants who were afraid, but Li Si and Zhao Gao as well. With their chief protector dead, they feared what an aroused public might do to them because of the strict reforms they had helped the emperor put in place. Hu Hai had good reason to be afraid, also. The First Emperor's eldest son and his personal choice for successor, Fu Su, had been banished because he objected to his father's treatment of the Confucian scholars. If Fu Su came back to claim the throne, he might very well take vengeance on family members who had not supported him.

On the journey back, therefore, the three conspirators secretly worked out a plan for a putting Hu Hai on the throne before the news of Shi Huangdi's death became widely known. Accordingly, they sent a letter to Fu Su, allegedly from his father, telling him that he was guilty of treason and that he should commit suicide. The obedient son did as he thought his father had commanded and took his own life, leaving the door open for Hu Hai to become Second Emperor.

THE QIN DYNASTY FALLS

Hu Hai reigned for three years, during which time intrigue at the court became increasingly tense and dangerous. In a power move, Zhao Gao managed to undermine the new emperor's confidence in Li Si, his chief minister, so that Li Si was arrested, tortured, and killed.

Zhao Gao then began manipulating the young emperor to make him doubt his own sanity. Bodde says that Zhao Gao "presented a deer to the Second Emperor in the court, but called it a horse. Most or all of the courtiers acquiesced in the deception [on pain of punishment], thus inducing the emperor to believe he was suffering from hallucinations."[75] The emperor then retreated to a remote palace for a rest, but Zhao Gao was not through with him. Bodde continues, "[Zhao Gao] engineered the appearance of a fake armed gang of 'bandit rebels.' In the ensuing disorder, which involved some fighting, the Second Emperor committed suicide."[76]

Zhao Gao now had the upper hand at the royal court, and he chose Zi Ying, a grandson of Shi Huangdi, to be the next ruler. Distrustful of Zhao Gao and afraid for his own safety, Zi Ying took the offensive. Not long after ascending the throne, he pretended to be ill. When Zhao Gao came to visit him, either Zi Ying himself or one of his aides stabbed Zhao Gao to death.

Meanwhile, outside of the royal court, rebellious groups had already started forming. In the winter of 207 B.C., the first band of rebels arrived at the capital under the leadership of a peasant chieftain named Liu Bang. When Zi Ying surrendered, Liu Bang spared his life and the lives of his family. He even refrained from destroying the city as was the usual custom of conquerors. However, when the main forces of the rebel army arrived at the capital, they killed the emperor and his family and burned the city to the ground.

Although fighting among competing rebel groups went on for several years after the fall of the Qin dynasty, it was the peasant chieftain, Liu Bang, who finally emerged victorious and established one of the most famous dynasties in Chinese history—the Han.

Chapter

6 The Former Han Dynasty: Rise of an Empire

The founder of the Han dynasty, Liu Bang, was an unusual type of ruler in ancient China. In the first place, he was a commoner with no aristocratic background. Early in his career, he had unintentionally become the leader of a group of bandits. Historians Yong Yap and Arthur Cotterell explain: "A man of obscure origins and illiterate, [Liu Bang] may have been forced into active rebellion by the rigor of [Qin] law. One tale relates how [Liu Bang], having lost a group of convicts and being doomed to execution for his failure of duty, fled and was made leader of a band of such fugitives."[77]

Sometime later, Liu Bang organized a rebel force to protest the oppressive regime of the Qin. Around 208 B.C., Liu Bang joined his own forces with a larger, more organized rebel army headed by Xiang Yu, a powerful nobleman from the state of Chu. Xiang Yu was commander of the rebel forces that burned the capital and killed the Qin imperial family after Liu Bang had already accepted their surrender and spared their lives.

Because of acts such as this, Liu Bang soon disagreed with his aristocratic commander and the two of them engaged in a four-year struggle for control of the empire. Although Xiang Yu's forces won most of the battles at the outset, Liu Bang's following steadily increased while that of Xiang Yu began to slacken. The highborn Xiang Yu had only contempt for the common people and could not imagine being beaten by one of them.

Xiang Yu died by his own hand at the age of thirty after being defeated in a desperate battle against Liu Bang's superior forces. H. G. Creel writes, "[Xiang Yu] was completely baffled by the fact that, although he led his men to victory after victory, his armies slowly melted away until he had to commit suicide."[78]

Following his victory over Xiang Yu in 202 B.C., Liu Bang became emperor. At first he refused the title, protesting that he had no distinguished lineage. But when his advisers and supporters pointed out that their titles would mean nothing without his, he agreed to accept the title. As was the Chinese custom, he then chose a name by which he wished to be known after his death—Gao Zu, meaning "High Progenitor," or forefather.

Though supreme ruler of a vast empire, Gao Zu's manner remained unpretentious throughout his reign. He never forgot his

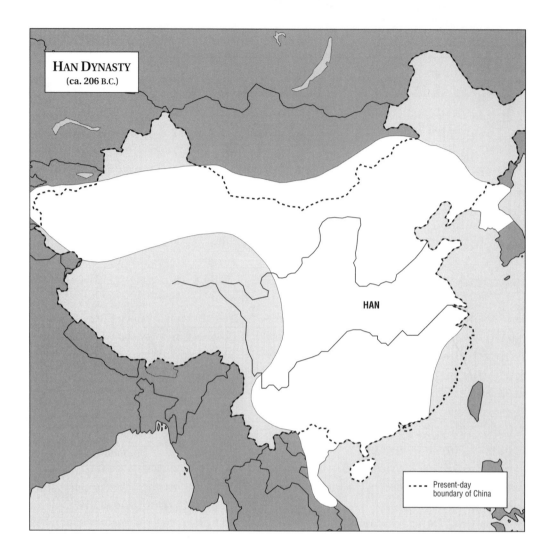

HAN DYNASTY
(ca. 206 B.C.)

HAN

- - - Present-day
boundary of China

humble beginnings and would periodically return to the town of his birth to visit his old friends. Commenting on Gao Zu's personality, historian Arthur Cotterell writes:

> Gaozu's mildness was a genuine part of his character, a single virtue in what was a very violent age, and it made his accession something of a popular

event. People felt that this commoner would govern in their interests, unlike the absolute rulers of Qin. On the throne he neither aped aristocratic manners nor slackened his compassion for his poorer subjects, and his habit of squatting down, coupled with an earthy vocabulary, unsettled polite courtiers and accentuated the kindly feeling of the people towards him.[79]

Gao Zu also had a more forgiving nature than his predecessors, bringing a less rigid attitude to the throne. Nevertheless, it would be a mistake to think of him as a genial, grandfatherly figure. Conquering formidable enemies and then taking over an immense empire required a certain amount of ruthlessness—a quality which he also possessed and drew on when the occasion called for it. "He fought by every means, fair or foul, that promised success," Creel writes. "He pledged his word and violated it as served his purpose."[80]

When the wars were over, he went about establishing his dynasty with the same determination.

REORGANIZING THE EMPIRE

Crude though he may have been, and possibly illiterate, Gao Zu was shrewdly intelligent and wise enough to know that he needed assistance in governing a large and diverse empire. Many of his policies were planned and carried out by his

---

A COURT OFFICIAL SPEAKS OUT

Unlike many other rulers, Emperor Gao Zu, an uneducated peasant who founded the Han dynasty, listened to his advisers and even allowed criticism of himself. In Records of the Historian, *translated by Burton Watson, Sima Qian records an important bit of advice given to the emperor by one of his envoys who had just returned from a successful mission.*

When Lu Chia returned and reported on his mission, Kao-tsu [Gao Zu] was greatly pleased and honored him with the rank of palace counselor. In his audiences with the emperor, Master Lu on numerous occasions expounded and praised the *Book of Odes* and the *Book of Documents*, until one day Kao-tsu began to rail at him. 'All I possess I have won on horseback!' said the emperor. 'Why should I bother with the *Odes* and *Documents*?'

'Your Majesty may have won it on horseback, but can you rule it on horseback?' asked Master Lu. 'Kings T'ang and Wu in ancient times won possession of the empire through the principle of revolt, but it was by the principle of obedience that they assured the continuance of their dynasties. To pay due attention to both civil and military affairs is the way for a dynasty to achieve long life.'

advisers, to whom he gave credit and even generous rewards. Gao Zu moderated the strict Legalism of the Qin dynasty by granting amnesty for prisoners, freeing slaves, lowering taxes, and doing away with excessive penalties, such as punishing entire families for crimes committed by one of their members.

Although Gao Zu favored these reforms, he nevertheless wanted to keep intact the centralized government set up during the Qin dynasty. However, there were two major obstacles to that goal. In the struggle to establish his dynasty, Gao Zu had allowed some generals to become kings over conquered territories, and he feared losing their support by taking their titles away from them. Moreover, he had to reward loyal family members and friends who expected royal titles and estates.

Since this system of rewards was very much like feudalism, to which Gao Zu did not wish to return, he and his advisers finally worked out a compromise. The newly created kings were allowed to reign, and family members and friends were granted traditional positions. At the same time many of the old Qin commanderies were left intact to be administered under officials directly responsible to the royal court.

Gao Zu knew this was a risky solution. Experience had proven that royal titles and special privileges, once granted, were hard to rescind. Therefore, Gao Zu took measures to see that these arrangements were only temporary. "Before the first emperor's reign was over," historian Ray Huang writes, "many of the marquises had already been found at fault and removed from their positions."[81] Under later emperors, all the territories were brought back under central control.

THE RISE OF CONFUCIANISM

Another challenge faced by the new emperor was reconciling the ideological struggle between competing theories of government, particularly between Legalism and Confucianism. Gao Zu recog-

The teachings of Confucius influenced Emperor Gao Zu to adopt a more moderate legal system and reduce the severity of punishments for those that violated the law.

nized that Legalism as an underlying philosophy had failed insofar as the people were concerned. Moreover, he understood that the teachings of Confucius were very popular among a large portion of the population. It would be several years before Confucianism would be officially accepted by the royal court, but Gao Zu opened the door for it as he did for many other political reforms that would take place in later times.

GAO ZU'S SUCCESSORS

The first Han emperor's reforms would prove to have a lasting impact on China. Gao Zu died in 188 B.C. after a reign of only seven years. Those years were dynamic ones, though, in which he set the tone for later rulers of his own dynasty and even of dynasties to come. His death brought about the usual scramble for succession with some very dramatic twists introduced by Gao Zu's wife, the Empress Lu.

The empress, who had married Gao Zu before he became emperor, bore their son, Liu Ying. After becoming emperor, Gao Zu also had children by several concubines, and he selected one of these sons as his successor. Empress Lu had other plans, however. After Gao Zu's death, she managed to get Liu Ying named emperor in spite of Gao Zu's wishes. When Liu Ying (whose imperial name was Hui Di) died at the age of twenty-three, Empress Lu acted as regent to her son's successors for several years thereafter.

Lu never took the title of ruling empress, but, as historian Michael Loewe observes, "Nonetheless, she held unquestioned authority. She nominated four members of her own family as kings. . . . She also elevated six of her kinsmen to marquis and appointed others to posts as generals."[82] When Lu died in 180 B.C., her family, grown powerful by her appointments, made a move to end the Liu line of succession within the Han dynasty.

They were thwarted, however, by a coalition of Gao Zu's heirs. The result was the enthroning of Gao Zu's grandson, Wen Di, as emperor, thus continuing the dynasty. In 141 B.C., Wen Di's great-grandson ascended the throne and became one of China's most esteemed rulers, Emperor Wu Di. The empire that Wu Di inherited from his forebears was internally strong but increasingly threatened from the outside by nomadic tribes. It would be Wu Di's job to counter this external threat.

THE REIGN OF EMPEROR WU DI

Wu Di was only fifteen years old when he became emperor and so, until he came of age, the empire was managed by regents and advisers. Influenced by the teachings of Confucius in his youth, Wu Di proclaimed Confucianism as the underlying principle of his government. His definition of Confucianism was very broad, however, and his personality was much more attuned to Legalism.

Wu Di worked hard at being emperor, and busily involved himself in all aspects of government. Through a large staff of writers, he issued hundreds of edicts on

Emperor Wu Di mounted a military campaign to eliminate the nomadic tribes that constantly harassed the empire's borders.

many subjects. Wu Di actively recruited outstanding young men to take examinations for government positions, and in 124 B.C. he established an imperial academy to prepare pupils to take the examinations.

BORDER WARS

Although Wu Di did not personally command troops as some emperors did, he nevertheless became known as the "martial emperor" because of the conquering armies he sent out. Wu Di, however, did take active part in planning military campaigns, the first of which was against the fierce nomadic Xiongnu tribes who inhabited the steppes in the northwest. Former emperors had dealt with the Xiongnu by building defensive walls and by alternately fighting with them and appeasing them.

Emperor Gao Zu's policy had been to buy off the tribes with valuable presents such as rice, silk, alcohol, and copper coins. He even sent a Chinese princess as a wife for one of the chieftains. However, when it was learned that the Xiongnu had formed an alliance of nomadic tribes against the Han, appeasement was no longer a viable alternative. Strong military action had to be taken.

The logistical problems of moving and supplying thousands of troops in such remote areas was staggering, but Wu Di put the resources of the empire behind the effort. As a man of great ambition, he used the border wars as a means to expand the empire, not just defend it. However, he did not rely on military might alone to bring the Han dynasty to unprecedented power. He was also a master of diplomacy, often using subtlety and persuasion to achieve his goals.

EXPANSION THROUGH TRADE AND DIPLOMACY

Although the time for diplomacy with the Xiongnu had passed, Wu Di thought it still might work with another nomadic tribe, the Yuezhi, who were enemies of the

An Emperor's Search for Talent

The great Han emperor Wu Di was always on the lookout for the best and brightest men to fill the offices of his administration. One of his recruitment methods was by public announcement, as in the following proclamation excerpted from China: Its History and Culture *by W. Scott Morton.*

HEROES WANTED! A PROCLAMATION

Exceptional work demands exceptional men. A bolting or a kicking horse may eventually become a most valuable animal. A man who is the object of the world's detestation may live to accomplish great things. As with the intractable horse so with the infatuated man;—it is simply a question of training.

We therefore command the various district officials to search for men of brilliant and exceptional talents, to be OUR generals, OUR ministers, and OUR envoys to distant States.

A cave painting of a Han general with his soldiers. Emperor Wu Di was constantly looking for bright and talented men to serve as generals, ministers, and envoys.

As shown in this painting of the Han in battle, warfare and military readiness were an integral part of the Han dynasty.

Xiongnu. He therefore sent a special envoy, General Zhang Qian, to locate the tribe and persuade them to join the Han in their military campaigns against the Xiongnu.

Before he was able to locate the Yuezhi, however, Zhang Qian was captured by the Xiongnu. After being held prisoner for ten years, he finally escaped and continued his mission to find the Yuezhi. He eventually located them far to the west in what today is Afghanistan. Although he stayed with the Yuezhi for a year, he was unable to persuade them to join an alliance to fight the Xiongnu, so in 126 B.C.

he returned to China to report to the emperor.

Wu Di was astonished to see him, of course, but even more surprised when he described the faraway places to which he had traveled and the exotic peoples he had met. The most exciting news for the emperor, however, was that Zhang Qian had seen Chinese goods, particularly silk, in remote places, no doubt transported there by tribal trading routes unknown to the royal court.

The fact that other peoples prized Chinese goods delighted Wu Di and set him thinking about the political and commercial possibilities of establishing trade routes in those areas. Encouraged by Zhang Qian's report, Wu Di later established a "silk road" along which Chinese goods traveled far and wide. To secure safe passage for caravans along these trading routes, the Han made pacts with tribes through which the route passed.

To insure that the pact agreements were kept, young tribal men were brought to the Han capital as hostages, but of a very different sort than that term usually implies. These hostages lived luxuriously and were treated with the utmost kindness. In exchange, Chinese princesses were sent as brides to tribal chieftains where they were expected to introduce Chinese culture to their new families.

Diplomatic arrangements such as these (backed up with Han military might when necessary) spread Chinese goods into areas far outside of China, including the present-day countries of India, Myanmar, Korea, and Afghanistan. Chinese silks even reached Rome, although the Chinese were never aware of that empire's existence.

Thus, by a combination of militancy and diplomacy, under the Han, China became wealthy and powerful, encompassing

Caravans traveling on the silk road, depicted in this cave painting, carried Chinese trade goods as far as ancient Rome.

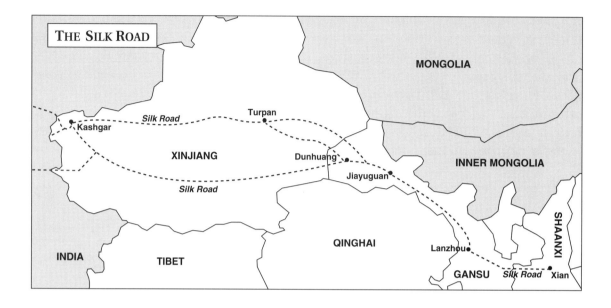

The Silk Road

almost as much territory as China does today. Moreover, a climate favorable for artistic and intellectual development was fostered during Former Han times, resulting in outstanding works of literature and art.

LITERARY ACHIEVEMENTS OF THE FORMER HAN

One of China's greatest literary classics, *Shih chi* (*Records of the Historian*), was written during the Former Han era by Sima Qian, a historian in the court of Wu Di. While writing the book, Sima Qian angered the emperor by disagreeing with him on a policy matter. Convicted of treason for his boldness, Sima Qian was sentenced to death, or punishment by castration. The humiliation of castration was felt to be worse than death by most men, and thus, it was customary for those under such a sentence to commit suicide. Sima Qian, however, desperately wanted to finish his history book, so he submitted to castration. "Two thousand years of admiring readers have amply rewarded his bitter decision,"[83] comments professor Burton Watson, translator of Sima Qian's history.

Sima Qian's work covers the entire history of China up to his own time. His research must have been extremely difficult, as reliable records were hard to find. Nevertheless, the book has been highly regarded by historians past and present, not only for its scholarship, but for its intimate glimpses of people and events.

Besides Sima Qian, many other gifted writers produced memorable works during the Former Han dynasty. One of these was Lu Chia, a Confucian scholar who served Emperor Gao Zu as adviser and ambassador. Lu Chia is noted for his political essays, collected in a book called *New Analects*.

A Distinguished Literary Work from Ancient China

One of the most respected literary works to come out of ancient China is Records of the Historian *by Sima Qian, written in the second century* B.C. *In the following excerpt, Grace S. Fong discusses this monumental work. Fong is quoted in* China: Ancient Culture, Modern Land, *edited by Robert E. Murowchick.*

The first great historian of China, Sima Qian (145?–90? BC), was active during the reign of Emperor Wu, one of the most powerful and able leaders in Chinese history. Sima Qian succeeded his father to the post of Grand Historian-Astrologer at court and completed the monumental historiographical project that they had begun together, the 'Records of the Historian.' It is an ambitious work that attempts to write the history of China from the earliest antiquity to the time of Emperor Wu. Not one of the early historical writings can equal it in scope and organization, innovative conception and style. The form and organization of the 'Records of the Historian' provided the model for all later dynastic histories and it has also been enjoyed as literature by generations of Chinese readers up to the present.

The 'Records of the Historian' consists of 130 chapters divided into five large sections: 'Basic Annals,' 'Chronological Tables,' 'Treatises,' 'Hereditary Houses,' and 'Biographies.' The materials and chapters within each of the five sections are arranged chronologically. The 'Biographies' section comprises 70 chapters and is by far the largest section of the work. It is also the most innovative in form and the most read and admired as both history and literature. For the first time in historical writing, the life and actions of an individual serve as the unifying focus for the development of theme and narrative. Although these chapters are not biographies in the sense of a detailed recounting of the life of a person that we expect to find in the modern form, his dramatized realizations of ancient historic personages, some of whom have been immortalized because of their representation in this work, demonstrate Sima Qian's skill.

A MELANCHOLY PRINCESS

Women in Chinese imperial circles were often used to secure political alliances with other noble families or even with distant tribes outside the Chinese perimeter. Such was the case of Princess Xi-chun, sent to be the bride of a nomadic chieftain by Emperor Wu Di in his relentless expansion of the empire. The following poem written by the forlorn princess is excerpted from World Poetry: An Anthology of Verse from Antiquity to Our Time, *edited by Katherine Washburn and John S. Major.*

Lament

My family married me off
to the King of the Wusun,
a million miles from nowhere.
My house is a tent.
My walls are of felt.
Raw flesh is all I eat,
with horse milk to drink.
I always think of home
and my heart stings.
O to be a yellow snow-goose
floating home again!

Another prominent writer during the Former Han was Chia I, a historian and poet. He was particularly renowned for his *fu* verses, a type of poetry that was popular during Han times. Composing poetry was a fashionable pastime among members of the Han upper classes. In fact, poetry was considered so important to a gentleman's education that candidates for governmental positions were often required to compose poems as part of their examinations.

Material from Han literature remains helpful in reconstructing the social and cultural framework of that period in history and provides confirmation of evi-dence collected elsewhere. In recent times, the literature of the Han, long known to scholars, has been dramatically supported with the discovery of several unplundered tombs dating to the Former Han period.

TREASURES FROM FORMER HAN TOMBS

In 1971 construction of a hospital threatened to destroy two unexcavated burial mounds in China's Hunan Province. The mounds were thought to be the burial places of a noble family of the tenth century. Upon excavation, however, archaeologists discovered three tombs lying beneath the mounds. From seals and inscriptions found inside the tombs, excavators were surprised to learn that the occupants had lived in the second century B.C., during the reign of Wu Di. They were identified as Li Cang, first marquis of Da, his wife, and their son. Da was a small principality in south central China during the Former Han.

In the first tomb to be excavated, archaeologists found the body of a woman in a set of nested coffins. She was swathed in silk and amazingly well preserved after two thousand years in the tomb. A wide array of grave goods surrounded the coffins, including wooden statuettes of servants to assist the lady in the afterlife. Substitution of wooden images in place of human sacrifices had begun earlier—Confucius had spoken approvingly of the trend—but the new practice had taken centuries to become firmly established.

Also among the grave goods were exquisite silk fabrics and garments, all woven and decorated with great skill. A banner of silk folded on top of the last coffin was embroidered with a fantasy-like scene, and layers of silk covered the woman's body. Another type of grave goods found in abundance in the tomb was lacquer ware—dishes, bowls, wine vessels, cups, and various kinds of containers. Lacquer ware, prized for its light weight and colorful appearance, had become very popular among the Han nobility. *National Geographic* staff writer Alice J. Hall describes its production:

In Han times artisans in small factories produced the lacquer ware, one of China's superlative inventions. Over a thin base of carved wood or woven bamboo, they applied successive coats of lacquer, the resin of a native sumac tree, building up a hard, acid-resistant surface. Powdered minerals added to the lacquer created vibrant colors. With flowing brush strokes, the craftsmen painted delicate flower petals,

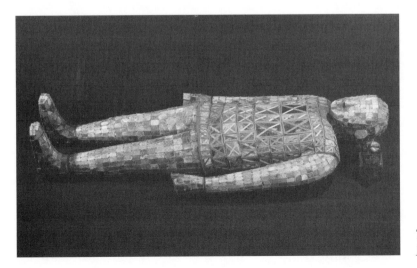

The jade burial suit of Princess Dou Wan.

grass blades, and clouds. The product, amazingly lightweight, became a popular trade item.[84]

Two other tombs dating back to the first century B.C. also testify to the skill of Han artisans. The tombs, hewn out of a rocky hillside in Hebei Province (north China), contained the remains of Prince Jing of Zhongshan and his wife Dou Wan. At their deaths, both bodies had been completely encased in suits made of small pieces of jade fastened together with gold threads. Modern artisans estimate that each suit would have taken ten years to complete, given the jade-working tools available in Han times. Grave goods in the tombs included silk garments, pottery, lacquer ware, and skillfully crafted items of bronze, jade, gold, and silver. The remains of six chariots were found in the prince's tomb.

The wealth displayed in tombs of relatively minor nobles and officials such as these demonstrates the enormous wealth attained in the Former Han. Such success was not achieved without price, however. The vast expenditures of Wu Di's government, coupled with the extravagant lifestyles of Han elite, began to put the economic base of the empire under severe strain.

THE HAN ECONOMY

Production of various goods such as iron and silk were very important in the Han economy, but the primary basis for supporting the empire was still agriculture.

Taxation of farmers and farm products supplied most of the money to run the empire, but there was a problem: Neither Wu Di nor any of the previous emperors had been able to prevent rich families from acquiring more and more land on which they paid little or no taxes. This left the poor farmers with less land to cultivate and more taxes to pay.

Wu Di tried to remedy these strains on the economy by creating government monopolies in liquor, salt, and iron. He also levied new taxes on merchants, and forced wealthy nobles to make gifts to the government. Though successful in the short run, the continuation of measures such as these required the hand of a strong leader with popular support. When Wu Di died in 87 B.C., his son and successor was only a boy, leaving a void that no one else was able to fill. The empire was once more subjected to the seething jealousies and sinister plots of the imperial court.

THE EMPIRE AFTER WU DI

Wu Di fathered children by two empresses and numerous consorts. When Wu Di died, Huo Guang, his chief minister, saw his chance to seize power by becoming regent to Wu Di's son Liu Fu-ling. The boy's mother, one of Wu Di's consorts, had already died. Liu Fu-ling, who became Emperor Zhao Di, did not rule for long, and died at the age of twenty-two. The next emperor chosen by Huo Guang lasted less than a month before being

DEATH OF A CONCUBINE

In ancient China, women could exercise political power only indirectly, as wives, mothers, and concubines to emperors and other noblemen. Concubines, chosen for their beauty, were in an especially delicate situation as they aged. This situation is dramatically presented in a book written in the first century A.D. The excerpt is taken from Courtier and Commoner in Ancient China: Selections from the History of the Former Han by Pan Ku, *translated by Burton Watson.*

Madam Li, Concubine of Emperor Wu

Madam Li bore him a son [who was made a king] . . . but died shortly afterwards at a very young age. . . . Earlier, when Madam Li lay critically ill, the emperor came in person to inquire how she was, but she pulled the covers over her face and, apologizing, said, "I have been sick in bed for a long time and my face is thin and wasted. I cannot let Your Majesty see me, though I hope you will be good enough to look after my son the king and my brothers."

"I know you've been very sick, and the time may come when you never rise again," said the emperor. "Wouldn't you feel better if you saw me once more and asked me face to face to take care of the king and your brothers?"

"A woman should not appear before her lord or her father when her face is not properly made up," she said. "I would not dare let Your Majesty see me in this state of disarray." . . .

When the emperor continued to insist on one last look at her, Madam Li, sobbing, turned her face toward the wall and would not speak again. The emperor rose from his seat in displeasure and left.

Madam Li's sisters berated her. "Why couldn't you let him have one look at you and entreat him face to face to take care of your brothers! Why should you anger him like this!"

"The reason I didn't want the emperor to see me," she said, "was so I could make certain he would look after my brothers! It was because he liked my looks that I was able to rise from a lowly position and enjoy the love and favor of the ruler. But if one has been taken into service because of one's beauty, then when beauty fades, love will wane, and when love wanes, kindness will be forgotten. The emperor thinks fondly and tenderly of me because he remembers the way I used to look. Now if he were to see me thin and wasted, with all the old beauty gone from my face, he would be filled with loathing and disgust and would do his best to put me out of his mind. Then what hope would there be that he would ever think kindly of me again and remember to take pity on my brothers?"

removed as unfit to rule. Next in line was Xuan Di, a descendant of one of Wu Di's empresses. Xuan Di was eighteen years old when he became emperor and he already had a wife and son.

Huo Guang, still acting as regent, wanted his daughter to become empress, but Xuan Di insisted on elevating his own wife to that position. This angered Huo Guang's wife, Huo Xien, who had the new empress poisoned. Her crime was not discovered until years later, however, and the Huo family remained firmly entrenched in the imperial court. After Huo Guang died, Huo Xien's crime was discovered. The Huo family was disgraced, and many of its members committed suicide or were executed.

Emperor Xuan Di survived the turmoil and capably ruled the empire for twenty-five years. He was succeeded by Yuan Di, the son born to him and his murdered wife before she became empress. Yuan Di was also a capable ruler who tried to deal with the growing economic crisis in the empire, but without great success. After Yuan Di's death in 33 B.C., infighting over imperial succession began again. Amid the chaos, Wang Mang, a powerful minister in the imperial court, forcibly took over the throne in A.D. 9.

AN USURPER ON THE THRONE

Although Wang Mang had ties to the royal family through one of the emperor's consorts, he was not in the direct line of descent and was thus considered a usurper. Nevertheless, as a man of considerable ability, he set about trying to solve the many problems besetting the empire. It was a task at which many others had failed, and Wang Mang was destined to do the same after fifteen years of rule.

During his reign, the empire gradually descended into chaos. Excessive taxation and terrible living conditions triggered widespread peasant uprisings. Conditions for the poor were made even worse when the Yellow River changed its course, displacing thousands of people and creating widespread famine.

On the other end of the social scale, the nobles, fearful of Wang Mang's efforts to break their power, banded together. "It was the combination of these two forces which finally won the day in 23," states historian Jacques Gernet. "After the defeat and death of the usurper, one of the representatives from the old Liu line from the region of Nanyang, in the south of Honan, assumed power and restored the Han dynasty."[85]

7 The Later Han Dynasty: Decline and Fall of the Empire

Following Wang Mang's death (a violent one in which he was beheaded), fourteen emperors occupied the throne during a period which historians call the Later Han to distinguish it from the Former Han when the empire was at its zenith. When Wang Mang was overthrown in A.D. 23, a scramble to restore the Han dynasty ensued among those who claimed a right to the throne. In 25, all opposition was crushed by Liu Xiu, whose military campaign had been supported by nobles and wealthy landowners opposed to Wang Mang's land reform policies. Liu Xiu was proclaimed emperor by his supporters, and thus the Han dynasty was restored after a fifteen-year interruption. The new emperor took the name Guang Wu Di.

Enthronement of the new emperor did not end the fighting, however, as other contenders for the throne continued to press their claims. Moreover, nomadic tribes on the empire's frontiers took advantage of the domestic turmoil to harass the border towns. Nevertheless, Guang Wu Di held firm and ruled the empire for thirty-two years.

RETURN TO FEUDALISM

One of Guang Wu Di's first acts as emperor was to move his capital away from Changan (present day Xian), where opposition to his rule was strong. He established his new capital at Luoyang, several miles east of Changan. Because of this move, historians sometimes refer to the two Han eras as Western Han (Former), and Eastern Han (Later).

During Wang Mang's short reign, he had broken up the estates of wealthy landowners and taken away many of their privileges. Since Guang Wu Di owed his military success to landowners, he could not alienate them by promoting land reform measures during his reign. Consequently, landowners regained their estates and privileges, and the empire slowly reverted to the feudalistic practices of past dynasties. Moreover, hard-won advances made by peasants, such as landownership and improved social status, began to slip away. Historians Yong Yap and Arthur Cotterell describe the situation as follows:

As a direct result of the throne's enforced neutrality on the land question a number of social developments took place during the Later Han. The *nung* [peasant farmers] lost most of their freedom, becoming dependent farmers on large estates. The economic condition of those whose land was less than one hundred *mou* [about twelve acres] . . . became intolerable. Debt forced them to sell their holdings. Two methods of livelihood then remained: they could stay on their land as share-croppers, paying fifty per cent of the harvest to their landlord, or, still worse, accept employment as wage labourers. . . . The corollary of this social downgrading of the *nung* was the formation of a quasi-feudal system.[86]

Peasants were not the only casualties of the return to feudalism. Government positions formerly open to anyone who could pass the examinations were gradually taken over by members of the privileged classes through appointment rather than merit. As privileges for the wealthy increased, powerful family clans began to set up semi-independent kingdoms, each

A modern depiction of Red Eyebrow rebels storming Changan, the imperial capital, in A.D 18.

with its own military force. As a result, the power of the imperial government diminished, leaving it vulnerable to a rising tide of armed rebellions from the peasantry.

PEASANT REBELLIONS

Although peasant rebellions were not new in China, they became more extensive and better organized during the Later Han era. Some dissident groups, headed by charismatic leaders and fired by religious fervor, evolved into major social movements.

One such group was the Red Eyebrows, whose name came from red marks painted on their foreheads to distinguish themselves from government forces. Born of desperation, the Red Eyebrow movement was composed of small groups of wandering peasants who had little to lose. "The common denominator that brought them together was starvation," writes professor Hans Bielenstein, "and the immediate objective that held them together in their wanderings was the urge to fill their bellies."[87]

A more highly organized peasant group, which emerged in eastern China around 170, was the Yellow Turbans. It was founded by a prominent Daoist leader, Zhang Zhiao, and his two brothers. The Yellow Turbans chose as their patron Huangdi, the Yellow Emperor of ancient times, thus giving rise to the group's name and the color of the headgear they wore. Members of the sect looked forward to the coming of a glorious new age, which they called the Great Peace. Eagerly embraced by impoverished peasants, the Yellow Turban movement rapidly grew in size and influence.

Another dissident peasant group in western China was known as the Five Bushels of Rice, the price of joining the organization. Like the Yellow Turbans, it was based on Daoist doctrines. Although popular in western China, it did not become as prominent or influential as the Yellow Turbans.

Hard pressed by rebellious peasants on one side and wealthy landholders on the other, the imperial government began to show signs of strain. The situation was made even worse by a series of weak emperors who sidestepped their responsibilities and delegated authority to court ministers. In Later Han times, many of the ministers who handled the affairs of state were eunuchs.

RISE OF THE EUNUCHS

Although emperors of the Later Han chose to rely on powerful ministers to run the empire, these aides posed a threat. A particularly ambitious minister could be tempted to overthrow the emperor and establish his own dynasty. The solution was to employ eunuchs as their closest advisers. Eunuchs were castrated men whose job originally was to look after the women of the court. Since castration made them incapable of producing offspring, the presence of eunuchs in the emperor's harem posed no threat to his royal lineage. However, living close to empresses, consorts, and their offspring, eunuchs exerted considerable influence in court policies and decisions.

Consorts and their families fiercely competed with one another for the emperor's favor, and many beleaguered emperors began to rely on eunuchs to handle the plots and counterplots constantly stirring in the imperial household. "In the Later Han period," Yap and Cotterell report, "eunuchs were used by the throne against the consort families, till they became a dangerous faction in their own right."[88]

Many eunuchs were men of high intelligence and administrative ability. Some of them were also opportunists who used their positions to advance their own interests. Court eunuchs even banded together to force concessions from the imperial court. Historian Jacques Gernet writes, "In 135 they [eunuchs] were authorized to adopt sons, and their power grew with their wealth. Owning large agricultural domains (the case is quoted of a eunuch who owned 32 houses and some 2500 acres of tilled land), they turned to big business and controlled their own slave workers."[89] Near the end of the Later Han era, the power of the eunuchs was finally broken, but by that time, the dynasty was already beyond saving.

Of the fourteen emperors who reigned during the Later Han dynasty, five were children who never reached their majority, and four of the adult emperors died before the age of thirty-four. Chinese historians gave high ratings to the first emperor, Guang Wu Di, and to his immediate successors, Ming Di and Zhang Di. All others were described as bad or worthless, mainly due to their neglect of the empire. Nevertheless, in spite of weak emperors and deteriorating social conditions, many noteworthy artistic and intellectual achievements were made in Later Han times.

LITERATURE OF THE LATER HAN DYNASTY

Learning was prized in China from early dynasties onward, with itinerant teachers gathering pupils wherever they could, in much the same way Confucius had. While these traveling teachers occasionally attracted students of modest means (Confucius, for example, never turned anyone away), formal education was mainly reserved for the elite classes. Always in demand were promising young men to fill the important positions in the government.

The training academy for officeholders established by Wu Di in the Former Han was supported and expanded by Later Han emperors. Historian Ray Huang reports, "In A.D. 59, [Emperor] Ming-di lectured on ancient history at the new imperial university at Loyang; the open session is said to have attracted a crowd of many thousands. In the second century A.D. this university had 240 buildings comprising 1,850 rooms. By the middle of the century . . . this institution had 30,000 students either enrolled at or affiliated with it."[90] Amid a political climate supportive of scholarly pursuits, many important literary works were created during the Later Han dynasty. These included

A COURT JESTER

Many Chinese emperors employed quick-witted courtiers in the manner of court jesters. Emperor Wu was especially fond of one Tung-fang Shuo, who often made him laugh. Shuo's amusing antics also helped him get away with brazen behavior, as shown in the following excerpt from Courtier and Commoner in Ancient China: Selections from the History of the Former Han by Pan Ku, *translated by Burton Watson.*

Tung-fang Shuo was rich in words, a man of jests and witticisms, an actor and a buffoon. . . . He had his stiff moods and his relaxed ones, his bobbings and his sinkings. So I [first-century historian Ban Gu] have transmitted the Biography of Tung-fang Shuo.

The emperor appointed Shuo a gentleman in constant attendance and eventually bestowed great affection and favor on him. Some time later, during the hottest days of summer, the emperor ordered that a gift of meat be given to his attendants. But, although the day grew late, the assistant to the imperial butler did not appear to distribute the gift. Shuo then took it upon himself to draw his sword and cut off a portion of the meat, saying to his fellow officials, "In these hot days one ought to go home early. With your permission, therefore, I will take my gift." Then he put the meat into the breast of his robe and went off. The imperial butler reported him to the emperor, and when Shuo appeared at court, the emperor said, "Yesterday when the gift of meat was being given out, you did not wait for the imperial command but cut off a piece of the meat with your sword and made away with it. What do you mean by such behavior!"

Shuo doffed his cap and apologized, but the emperor said, "Stand up, sir, and confess your faults."

Shuo bowed twice and said, "All right now, Shuo! You accepted the gift without waiting for the imperial command—what a breach of etiquette! You drew your sword and cut the meat—what singular daring! When you carved it up, you didn't take much—how abstemious [sparing] of you! You took it home and gave it to the little lady—how big-hearted!"

The emperor laughed and said, "I told you to confess your faults and here you are praising yourself!" Then he presented him with a further gift of a gallon of wine and a hundred catties [about 130 pounds] of meat and told him to take them home to "the little lady."

dictionaries and encyclopedias, commentaries on Chinese classical literature, philosophical treatises, fictional tales, poetry, songs, and histories.

One of the histories written during the Later Han dynasty, *Han Shu*, or *History of the Former Han*, became a Chinese classic. It was written by Ban Gu, a scholar from a prominent family. His personal story is similar to that of Sima Qian, but with a happier ending. Ban Gu's father was a noted intellectual who had begun writing the history of China where Sima Qian left off over a century before.

At his father's death, Ban Gu took over the task of completing the work with the assistance of his learned sister, Ban Zhao. However, instead of writing a broad history as Sima Qian had done, Ban Gu concentrated only on the history of the Former Han, starting with the reign of the first Han emperor, Gao Zu, and continuing through that of the usurper Wang Mang.

Ban Gu lived during the reign of Emperor Ming (A.D. 58–77) after Wang Mang had been deposed and the Han dynasty restored. When Emperor Ming got word that Ban Gu was writing about the Han dynasty, he was worried that the name of his family might be slandered. He therefore had Ban Gu arrested and his work confiscated.

Ban Gu's story then took a favorable turn, as Burton Watson explains: "When [Emperor Ming] examined [Ban Gu's] writings . . . he revised his opinion and not only released the historian but appointed him to a post in the imperial archives and encouraged him to continue his literary labors. [Ban Gu] was thus given access to government files and was allowed to complete the writing of his history under highly favorable circumstances."[91]

Ban Gu's history was published around the year 80 and was well received even in its own day. No one knows how much of the *Han Shu* was written by Ban Zhao, but the fact that a woman was given credit at all is highly unusual for that time.

A WOMAN SCHOLAR FROM THE LATER HAN

Fortunately for Ban Zhao, she was born into a family that provided academic education for their daughters as well as their sons. Otherwise her talents may not have been recognized in an era when women generally were not encouraged to be scholars. Through her distinguished family, she became a friend of the empress and served as an adviser and tutor to the women of the royal court. Besides assisting her brother with the history book, she also wrote a number of other works under her own name. One of these, *Lessons for Women*, is a small book of instructions on proper behavior for highborn ladies.

Although Ban Zhao accepted the Confucianist tradition of men controlling and women serving, she began to question the inequalities of education for the sexes. In *Lessons for Women*, she addressed this problem:

Works such as this funerary sculpture of entertainers show pleasurable pastimes during the Later Han.

Now examine the gentlemen of the present age. They only know that wives must be controlled, and that the husband's rules of conduct manifesting his authority must be established. They therefore teach their boys to read books and (study) histories. But they do not in the least understand that husbands and masters must (also) be served, and that the proper relationship and the rites should be maintained.

Yet only to teach men and not to teach women,—is that not ignoring the essential relationship between them?

According to the "Rites" [a book of proper social behavior] it is the rule to begin to teach children to read at the age of eight years, and by the age of fifteen years they ought then to be ready for cultural training. Only why should it not be (that girls' education as well as boys') be according to this principle?[92]

Ban Zhao also wrote poetry, a literary form popular in China from ancient times to the present. Poetry in Han times was written in several formal styles, each with a specified number of lines and beats per line. Some styles were very stiff and artificial, but other poems were simple outpourings from the heart, and often set to music. "From the beginning," writes historian Charles O. Hucker, "... Chinese poetry had a close relationship with music.... Most poetry was originally meant to be sung, or at least chanted in semimusical fashion."[93]

Outstanding works of visual art were also created during Later Han times. Although a great deal of Han art has been lost to grave robbers and conquering armies (the archives and collections at Luoyang were sacked and burned in A.D. 190), a number of outstanding examples of the work of Later Han artisans has been rescued from tombs dating to that period.

CREATIVE ARTS FROM LATER HAN TOMBS

In the highly prosperous Han dynasty, the accumulation of great wealth was not confined to the nobility. Commercial enterprises created many wealthy merchant families that more closely resembled business corporations than groups of people related by blood. Many of these families, whose members often held imperial offices as well, lavished enormous amounts of riches on their tombs.

Of great historical significance are paintings and low-relief sculptures that decorate the walls of many later Han tombs, which were lined with bricks or stone. Some of these decorations illustrate

The wealth of the Han nobility is indicated by fineries like this ornamented banner found in one of their tombs.

battles or other historical events; others depict domestic life and pleasurable pastimes. Han tombs also contained an abundance of small pottery figures that twentieth-century archaeologists find helpful in reconstructing everyday life in Han times. These include figures of people going about their daily tasks, various kinds of animals, and models of houses and other buildings. Small terra-cotta soldiers also have been found in great numbers, though smaller and much less realistic than those of Emperor Shi Huangdi's mausoleum.

In 1969 a spectacular cache of bronze sculptures was discovered in Gansu Province in northwest China. Dozens of small bronze statues of horses, carriages, and drivers (between ten and twenty inches high) were found in the tomb of a Later Han general. Among them was a galloping horse with one foot balanced on the back of a flying swallow. Now known as the "flying horse," or "horse and swallow," this sculpture has become a symbol of Later Han artistry. "Only a great master could have a conception at once so bold and logical," archaeologists Qian Hao,

Figurines from Han tombs show the amazing skill and attention to detail of the artisans of the Later Han era.

Chen Heyi, and Ru Suichu say of the unknown artist. "The 'horse and swallow' is an inspired example."[94]

The creativity of the Later Han era was by no means limited to art and literature, however, as it was also a time of scientific and technological innovation.

LATER HAN SCIENCE AND TECHNOLOGY

Although scientific inquiry was still closely akin to the occult—watching for natural omens, for instance, or searching for eternal life—some of the work done by Han intellectuals had scientific implications. Chinese astronomers began charting sun spots in 28 B.C., and Daoist magicians were experimenting with magnetism in the first century A.D. A seismograph was invented around A.D. 130 by Zhang Heng, head of the imperial observatory.

Many innovations were made in industrial technology as well. Improved machines for spinning and weaving silk made it possible to produce thousands of pounds of silk per year. Rolls of silk were often used in trade, and also became one of the most prized gifts with which Han emperors appeased the tribes on their borders. In A.D. 31, a water-powered blast furnace that produced temperatures high enough to turn iron into steel was introduced. Paper was another important invention that became a major industry in Later Han times. A coarse type of paper appeared during the Former Han, but by the second century A.D., high-quality paper was being produced in large rolls.

Mechanical inventions also boosted the salt industry. Salt had long been procured from the ocean and from lakes and marshes, but in Later Han times it was also obtained by drilling deep wells to tap underground brine. The brine was then brought to the surface through a network of bamboo pipes and evaporated in large iron containers.

Agriculture was the beneficiary of many innovations such as iron plows and water-powered milling tools for processing grain. The wheelbarrow, appropriately called the wooden ox, was invented. This relatively simple device was an enormous boon to farmers who had heretofore carried loads on their backs or in baskets suspended from shoulder yokes. Improvements in agriculture came not only from inventions, but also from advanced farming techniques such as terracing and contour plowing to prevent erosion.

Ground transportation was improved with new types of harnesses and collars for draft horses, enabling them to pull heavier loads with less effort. Water transportation was made safer and more efficient with the invention of a stern rudder for ships. Because the new rudder made steering easier, larger, more stable ships could be constructed.

In the field of medicine, important steps were taken toward shifting medical practices from the realm of magic to that of scientific inquiry. For example, acupuncture, a popular medical treatment in Later Han times, required an understanding of human anatomy and physiology. In earlier dynasties, those studies were hampered by a strict ban on the dissection of human

THE WEALTHY FAMILIES OF HAN TIMES

According to historian Charles O. Hucker, the traditional meaning of the word family *falls far short of describing the rich families of the Han dynasty. In the following excerpt from his book* China's Imperial Past, *Hucker explains what a well-to-do Han family was really like.*

The great families of Han times were not really groups of relatives. As a matter of fact, the [Qin] dynasty's policy of trying to destroy the great lineages and extended families of the [Zhou] tradition was continued under the Han dynasty. Relatives were actually discouraged from living together in extended families; for even three generations to live together in one household was considered remarkable in Later Han. The great Han family was something like a business company. The components of such a unit typically included (1) a wealthy, politically influential landholder; (2) his immediate family and household, including concubines, servants, and slaves; (3) his agricultural estate, probably including some scattered plots worked by tenants but ordinarily consisting mainly of a large, consolidated tract worked by serf-like indentured peasants and often partly by slaves; (4) a host of 'guests' ranging from astrologers and scholarly proteges to political spies and assassins; and (5) an army of private fighting men, who often manned castle-like fortifications that defended the estate from intruders. . . .

Especially in Later Han and Three kingdoms times, a great family of this type was a colossal enterprise. It might control thousands of acres, incorporating dozens of farm villages, mines and workshops, mills, and other industrial and commercial enterprises. Its 'guests' might number in the hundreds, its slaves in the thousands, and its fighting men in the tens of thousands. By any standard it was fabulously rich.

corpses. However, during the Later Han period, the bodies of executed criminals were allowed to be used for that purpose.

The good times did not last, however. While artists, scientists, philosophers, and inventors pursued their areas of interest, many longstanding problems—political, economic, and social—were rapidly merging into a series of events that would soon bring down the dynasty.

Fall of the Later Han Dynasty

For decades, imperial troops had put down intermittent peasant revolts, but in 184, the Yellow Turbans, with a force of three hundred thousand men, staged massive revolts in several regions around the capital. The rebels eventually were defeated by the imperial armies, but only after months of fighting. Afterward, smaller rebellions inspired by the Yellow Turbans continued to break out at various places in the empire.

A new crisis occurred in 189 when the imperial court was shattered by an internal issue involving palace eunuchs, who now numbered in the hundreds. Certain coalitions within the court plotted to kill the eunuchs, blaming them for the deterioration of the dynasty. Other court factions supported them, knowing they were not wholly to blame for the dynasty's woes.

Realizing they were in great danger, the palace eunuchs banded together and killed a general of the imperial army who was seeking their execution. They then took the emperor hostage and barricaded themselves in the palace. "On 25 September [189]," historian B. J. Mansvelt Beck reports, "Yuan Shao [an army colonel] broke into the palace compound and let his soldiers kill every eunuch in sight, reportedly over two thousand men."[95]

Although the dynasty officially lasted for several years after the massacre of the eunuchs, its effectiveness was at an end.

In 220, the last Han emperor, Xien Di, abdicated and the empire split into three kingdoms, each proclaiming its leader to be the rightful heir to the Han throne.

So prestigious had the house of Han become that leaders of the warring factions did not seek to overturn the dynasty; rather, each claimed to be the rightful successor to the Han throne. When none of them was able to gain supremacy, however, the empire fragmented. For the next four hundred years, numerous kingdoms rose and fell before another dynasty emerged with the strength to pull the empire back together.

Legacy of the Han Dynasty

During the Han dynasty, the basis upon which future dynasties would build was firmly established. Moreover, the hope that China would become reunited stubbornly persisted, even during the chaotic centuries that followed the dynasty's collapse. Historian Stephen Haw observes:

> It is a tribute to the strength of the Chinese identity established under the Han that such reunification was a constant aim throughout the period of disunion. Throughout its long history, the vast area of China had been difficult to govern (particularly in the era before modern communications), and has shown a recurring tendency to split into smaller states, yet the ideal of a united China has never faded.[96]

Disunity, Conflict, and Reunion

For historians, the fall of the Han dynasty marks the end of ancient history in China. The end of the Han ushered in a period of instability. The centuries that followed, however, were less violent than the Warring States period. Historian Ray Huang writes of the close of the Han age, "Although warfare was incessant in these centuries, large-scale engagements and decisive battles did not occur very often. . . . Clearly this was not another Warring States period. After four and a half centuries of imperial rule, China was no longer the same combination of competitive states grown out of feudal matrices [frameworks]."[97]

For the most part, life went on as before, especially for the common people. The attitude of Chinese peasants toward the quarrels of their rulers is simply but eloquently expressed in a folksong dating back to the Xia:

> At sunrise I rise to work,
> At sunset I return to rest.
> I drink from the well I dug,
> I eat from the yield of the field I tilled,
> The power of the emperor—
> What has that got to do with me?[98]

At times, of course, the power of the emperor had a lot to do with commoners who were recruited to build the defenses and fight the battles. Nevertheless, it was the persistent hope of a reunited Chinese empire among commoners and rulers alike that kept this difficult period from becoming a time of ignorance and fearful superstition.

The Han's empire split into three kingdoms, and attempts were made by each to establish hegemony over the others. Being of roughly equal strength, however, it was a long time before one of them succeeded. Finally, in 263, the northern kingdom of Wei, under the leadership of General Sima Zhao, conquered the southwest kingdom of Han Shu.

General Sima's son subdued the southeast kingdom of Wu in 280, bringing the empire together again in the process. The victors then proclaimed a new dynasty, the Jin. Unfortunately, the Jin empire was short-lived. Huang explains:

> With its seizure of Nanjing in 280, it apparently was on its way to realizing an imperial order in its full dimension. But hope was dashed only a

THE LEGACY OF THE SHORT-LIVED SUI DYNASTY

Although the Sui dynasty lasted only thirty-seven years, its contribution to the subsequent history of China was crucial, according to historian Arthur F. Wright. Wright sums up the legacy of the Sui in the following excerpt from his book The Sui Dynasty: The Unification of China, A.D. 581–617.

In the history of any civilization there appear times of relative stability, relative quiescence. And scattered through the records are periods of rapid change, of momentous innovation when old institutions are swept away and new solutions to old, intractable problems are found and put into effect. Such periods strike the historian, surveying the whole record of that civilization, as having been decisive for the distinctive shape which that civilization assumed. For the historian of Chinese civilization the Sui period, 581 to 617, is one of these. The Sui swept away the anachronistic institutions which had developed over the four centuries of disunion that preceded it. It replaced them with institutions that were the bone and sinew of the second great Chinese empire, The T'ang, that was to last until 906. . . . More than this, the Sui found ways to end the long centuries of separate political and cultural development in the four main regions of China, ways to ameliorate the cultural dissonance and disharmony, the mutual suspicion that had grown up in those separate regions.

Cave paintings such as this one depict life during the short-lived Sui dynasty.

Massive relief sculptures like this were created during the Tang dynasty.

decade later as events in north China began to rock the foundations of this promising dynasty. In 291 a domestic quarrel started within the Sima family, and the involvement of the imperial princes spread the strife from the palace to the countryside.[99]

A period of civil war followed during which a number of nomadic tribes took advantage of the chaos and broke through the old defenses to set up kingdoms of their own. At one time there were as many as sixteen kingdoms in the north, and four or five more in the south. Not until the sixth century was reunification accomplished once more.

"At last," historian Stephen Haw reports, "a general appeared [Yang Jian] who was able to conquer all of north China, establishing the Sui dynasty in 581, and then to overrun the south. By 589 the new dynasty controlled most of China, and by 610 had even brought part of Vietnam and large areas in Central Asia under its rule. Never again was China to undergo such a long period of disunity and confusion."[100]

Like the Qin dynasty that first united China, the Sui dynasty was of short duration, lasting only thirty-seven years. But, also like the Qin, it pulled the empire together after centuries of disunity. The Sui dynasty's successor, the Tang, not only continued to hold China together for the next three hundred years, but created an empire that eclipsed even the glorious Han.

Notes

Introduction: The First Dynasties

1. Derk Bodde, "The State and Empire of Ch'in," in Denis Twitchett and Michael Loewe, eds., *The Cambridge History of China,* vol. 1, *The Ch'in and Han Empires 221 B.C.–A.D. 220.* Cambridge, England: Cambridge University Press, 1986, pp. 57–58.

2. Christopher Hibbert, *The Emperors of China.* Chicago: Stonehenge Press, 1981, p. 15.

Chapter 1: The Xia Dynasty: Mythical or Real?

3. Edmund Capon and William Mac-Quitty, *Princes of Jade.* New York: E. P. Dutton, 1973, p. 28.

4. K. C. Wu, *The Chinese Heritage.* New York: Crown, 1982, p. 76.

5. Wu, *The Chinese Heritage,* p. 106.

6. Wu, *The Chinese Heritage,* pp. 116–17.

7. Quoted in Wu, *The Chinese Heritage,* p. 124.

8. Wu, *The Chinese Heritage,* p. 121.

9. Kwang-chih Chang, "Ritual and Power," in Robert E. Murowchick, ed., *China: Ancient Culture, Modern Land.* Norman: University of Oklahoma Press, 1995, p. 69.

10. W. Scott Morton, *China: Its History and Culture.* 3rd ed. New York: McGraw-Hill, 1995, p. 14.

11. Robert Silverberg, *Frontiers in Archeology.* Philadelphia: Chilton Books, 1966, pp. 56–57.

12. Caroline Blunden and Mark Elvin, *Cultural Atlas of China.* New York: Facts On File, 1983, p. 54.

13. Wu, *The Chinese Heritage,* p. 141.

Chapter 2: The Shang Dynasty: Rise of Chinese Civilization

14. Kwang-chih Chang, "Ritual and Power," p. 67.

15. Kwang-chih Chang, "Ritual and Power," p. 67.

16. Blunden and Elvin, *Cultural Atlas of China,* p. 56.

17. Silverberg, *Frontiers in Archeology,* p. 79.

18. Patricia Buckley Ebrey, *Cambridge Illustrated History of China.* Cambridge, England: Cambridge University Press, 1996, p. 25.

19. Ma Chengyuan, "The Splendor of Ancient Chinese Bronzes," in Wen Fong, ed., *The Great Bronze Age of China.* New York: Knopf, 1980, p. 5.

20. Silverberg, *Frontiers in Archeology,* p. 81.

21. Ebrey, *Cambridge Illustrated History of China,* p. 34.

22. Ebrey, *Cambridge Illustrated History of China,* p. 25.

23. Blunden and Elvin, *Cultural Atlas of China,* pp. 73–74.

24. *China's Buried Kingdoms.* Alexandria, VA: Time-Life Books, 1993, p. 25.

25. Hibbert, *The Emperors of China,* p. 13.

26. Kwang-chih Chang, "Ritual and Power," pp. 68–69.

Chapter 3: The Western (Early) Zhou Dynasty: Peaceful Interlude

27. Robert W. Bagley, "The Rise of the Western Zhou Dynasty," in Fong, *The Great Bronze Age of China,* p. 194.

28. Ebrey, *Cambridge Illustrated History of China*, p. 32.

29. Bagley, "The Rise of the Western Zhou Dynasty," p. 195.

30. Bagley, "The Rise of the Western Zhou Dynasty," p. 195.

31. Ebrey, *Cambridge Illustrated History of China*, p. 33.

32. Blunden and Elvin, *Cultural Atlas of China*, p. 60.

33. Blunden and Elvin, *Cultural Atlas of China*, p. 60.

34. Bagley, "The Rise of the Western Zhou Dynasty," p. 199.

35. Morton, *China*, pp. 31–32.

36. Bagley, "The Rise of the Western Zhou Dynasty," p. 197.

37. Yong Yap and Arthur Cotterell, *The Early Civilization of China*. New York: G. P. Putnam's Sons, 1975, p. 46.

38. Blunden and Elvin, *Cultural Atlas of China*, p. 184.

39. Milton W. Meyer, *China: A Concise History*. Lanham, MD: Rowman & Littlefield, 1994, p. 137.

40. David N. Keightley, "Sacred Characters," in Murowchick, *China: Ancient Culture, Modern Land*, p. 79.

41. Silverberg, *Frontiers in Archeology*, p. 84.

42. Morton, *China*, p. 24.

43. Yap and Cotterell, *The Early Civilization of China*, p. 35.

Chapter 4: The Eastern (Late) Zhou: Conflict and Creativity

44. Stephen Haw, *China: A Cultural History*. London: B. T. Batsford, 1990, p. 53.

45. Haw, *China*, p. 53.

46. Jacques Gernet, *A History of Chinese Civilization*. Cambridge, England: Cambridge University Press, 1982, p. 65.

47. Quoted in Morton, *China*, p. 26.

48. *China's Buried Kingdoms*, p. 50.

49. Haw, *China*, p. 54.

50. Ebrey, *Cambridge Illustrated History of China*, p. 41.

51. Morton, *China*, p. 26.

52. Ebrey, *Cambridge Illustrated History of China*, p. 53.

53. Samuel B. Griffith, trans., *Sun Tzu: The Art of War*. London: Oxford University Press, 1963, pp. 106–107.

54. Haw, *China*, p. 55.

55. H. G. Creel, *Chinese Thought: From Confucius to Mao Tse-Tung*. Chicago: University of Chicago Press, 1953, pp. 25–26.

56. Quoted in Creel, *Chinese Thought*, p. 42.

57. Yap and Cotterell, *The Early Civilization of China*, p. 64.

58. Creel, *Chinese Thought*, p. 45.

59. Ebrey, *Cambridge Illustrated History of China*, p. 47.

60. Eva Wong, *Lieh-Tzu: A Daoist Guide to Practical Living*. Boston: Shambala, 1995, p. 4.

61. Quoted in William Theodore de Bary, ed., *Sources of Chinese Tradition*, vol. 1. New York: Columbia University Press, 1960, p. 127.

Chapter 5: The Qin Dynasty: Unification and Imperialism

62. Gernet, *A History of Chinese Civilization*, p. 72.

63. Yap and Cotterell, *The Early Civilization of China*, p. 47.

64. Ebrey, *Cambridge Illustrated History of China*, p. 51.

65. Arthur Cotterell, *China: A Cultural History*. New York: Meridian, 1988, p. 66.

66. Gernet, *A History of Chinese Civilization*, p. 81.

67. Ray Huang, *China: A Macro History*. Armonk, NY: M. E. Sharpe, 1988, p. 32.

68. Bodde, "The State and Empire of Ch'in," p. 56.

69. Bodde, "The State and Empire of Ch'in," p. 51.

70. Haw, *China*, p. 66.

71. Bodde, "The State and Empire of Ch'in," p. 71.

72. Morton, *China*, p. 49.

73. Quoted in Arthur Cotterell, *The First Emperor of China*. New York: Holt, Rinehart, and Winston, 1981, p. 60.

74. Cotterell, *The First Emperor of China*, p. 60.

75. Bodde, "The State and Empire of Ch'in," p. 84.

76. Bodde, "The State and Empire of Ch'in," p. 56.

Chapter 6: The Former Han Dynasty: Rise of an Empire

77. Yap and Cotterell, *The Early Civilization of China*, p. 78.

78. Creel, *Chinese Thought*, p. 161.

79. Cotterell, *China*, p. 92.

80. Creel, *Chinese Thought*, p. 162.

81. Huang, *China*, p. 37.

82. Michael Loewe, "The Former Han Dynasty," in Twitchett and Loewe, *The Cambridge History of China*, vol. 1, p. 124.

83. Burton Watson, trans., *Records of the Historian: Chapters from the Shih chi of Ssu-ma Ch'ien*. New York: Columbia University Press, 1969, pp. 209–10.

84. Alice J. Hall, "A Lady from China's Past," *National Geographic*, May 1974, p. 675.

85. Gernet, *A History of Chinese Civilization*, p. 151.

Chapter 7: The Later Han Dynasty: Decline and Fall of the Empire

86. Yap and Cotterell, *The Early Civilization of China*, pp. 94–95.

87. Hans Bielenstein, "Wang Mang, the Restoration of the Han Dynasty, and Later Han," in Twitchett and Loewe, *The Cambridge History of China*, vol. 1, p. 244.

88. Yap and Cotterell, *The Early Civilization of China*, p. 85.

89. Gernet, *A History of Chinese Civilization*, p. 154.

90. Huang, *China*, p. 50.

91. Burton Watson, trans., *Courtier and Commoner in Ancient China: Selections from the History of the Former Han by Pan Ku*. New York: Columbia University Press, 1974, p. 4.

92. Nancy Lee Swann, *Pan Chao: Foremost Woman Scholar of China*. New York: Russell and Russell, 1968, pp. 84–85.

93. Charles O. Hucker, *China's Imperial Past: An Introduction to Chinese History and Culture*. Stanford, CA: Stanford University Press, 1975, p. 107.

94. Qian Hao, Chen Heyi, and Ru Suichu, *Out of China's Earth: Archaeological Discoveries in the People's Republic of China*. New York: Harry N. Abrams, 1981, p. 142.

95. B. J. Mansvelt Beck, "The Fall of Han," in Twitchett and Loewe, *The Cambridge History of China*, vol. 1, p. 345.

96. Haw, *China*, p. 81.

Epilogue: Disunity, Conflict, and Reunion

97. Huang, *China*, p. 62.

98. Quoted in Wu, *The Chinese Heritage*, p. 96.

99. Huang, *China*, p. 65.

100. Haw, *China*, p. 84.

Glossary

ancestor worship: A religious system in which the dead are believed to inhabit a spirit world where they are able to influence the living. Homage is therefore paid to them in the form of gifts and sacrifices to maintain their goodwill.

Anyang: An area in north central China which was the homeland of the Shang dynasty from about 1600 B.C. to 1050 B.C. Many important archaeological discoveries have been made there including treasure-filled tombs and thousands of oracle bones. Anyang is a large city in that area today.

Bronze Age: A division used by archaeologists and historians to differentiate Stone Age peoples from societies using tools and weapons made of bronze, an alloy of tin and copper. The traditional date for the beginning of the Bronze Age in China is about 2000 B.C.

Chinese dialects: Dialects are variations within a single language family that exhibit differences in speech patterns, vocabulary, and pronunciation. Chinese is divided into at least seven major language families, each of which is further divided into dialects. Variations in dialects are often so great, speakers of different dialects cannot understand one another.

Chinese writing: A logographic system of writing (nonalphabetic) which combines stylized pictures of objects to form logos or words. For example, a simple represen-

tation of a man kneeling before an altar means "to pray." Written Chinese has thousands of logos or characters. Unlike English, Chinese writing is not connected with speech.

concubine: A woman who has a legitimate sexual union with a man in societies allowing polygyny (men with multiple mates), but whose status is not as high as that of a wife. *Consort* is a similar term. The rules governing such practices differ according to time and place.

Confucius: A Chinese philosopher born in 552 B.C. whose teachings of virtue and upright living have had tremendous influence on Chinese political and social life. Although he wrote no books, his followers collected his sayings into a volume called *Analects*.

conscription: The practice of drafting laborers for public works or soldiers for military duty without their consent.

Daoism (also Taoism): An ancient Chinese philosophy that came into prominence during the Zhou dynasty. Its founder is Laozi who taught that striving for wealth and power is futile. Contentment lies in surrendering to the Dao, the mystical cosmic force of nature. Daoists believed governments should operate minimally and not interfere with peoples' lives.

dragon bones: Ancient animal bones considered to have healing properties. They were often dug up by farmers and sold to apothecary shops (drug stores) to be ground up in medicines.

dynasty: A succession of rulers from the same lineage.

Erlitou culture: An early Bronze Age culture that preceded the Shang dynasty and which some scholars have suggested may be the Xia dynasty.

eunuch: A castrated male who was assigned to the women's quarters of imperial households. Meant only to be domestic servants, many eunuchs nevertheless wielded great political power through their close connections with empresses, concubines, and the children of rulers.

halberd: An axlike weapon made of metal, particularly bronze, and mounted on a long shaft.

Han dynasty: The dynasty that overthrew the Qin dynasty and lasted about four hundred years (206 B.C.–A.D. 221). Noted for its cultural accomplishments as well as its military might, it is divided by historians into the Former Han, when the empire was strong and powerful, and the Later Han, when it began to decline.

hegemony: Leadership or dominance by a state that manages to bring other states or political units under its influence. A hegemon is the ruler or leader of such a coalition.

Huangdi (Yellow Emperor): A revered figure in Chinese history and folklore. Huangdi, also known as the Yellow Emperor, ruled long and wisely in a shadowy era preceding the first dynasty. Whether Huangdi is a mythical figure or a real person whose personal skills were exaggerated is unknown.

Legalism: A political philosophy that came to prominence during the Warring States period of the Zhou dynasty as an alternative to feudalism. Legalism called for a tightly controlled central government with administrative offices held by qualified persons. Legalism justified the right of rulers to exercise autocratic control. Its principle proponent was Han Feizi.

metallurgy: The process of mining, extracting, and smelting ores (tin, copper, gold, etc.) to be used in the production of artistic works, tools, weapons, and other useful items.

myth: Stories of people, animals, events, etc. having little or no factual basis. Myths have various uses such as explaining the unknown, illustrating a moral principle, making a point, celebrating heroes and heroines, or even instilling fear.

Neolithic: Literally, New Stone Age. The Neolithic Age is characterized by the appearance of farming and domestication of animals, resulting in settled communities and a more complex way of life than in the preceding Paleolithic Age. The Neolithic Age ended when metal replaced stone for tools and weapons.

oracle bones: Tortoise plastrons (undershells) and cattle scapula (shoulder blades) used to foretell the future by producing cracks on them with a hot iron. Hundreds of oracle bones were discovered in Shang dynasty sites with Chinese characters written on them, the first known Chinese writing.

Paleolithic: Literally, Old Stone Age. A pre-agricultural, pre-metal stage of human development during which people lived a nomadic lifestyle of hunting and gathering. The Paleolithic age is by far the longest era in human history.

piece-mold casting: The principal method of bronze casting during the Shang and Zhou dynasties. Bronze pieces were first sculpted in clay and molds were made from the clay model into which molten bronze was poured. Many of the bronze works of that age were so complex, they were molded in separate pieces and then fitted together.

pinyin: A system for romanizing Chinese into English. In 1979 it became the official system used by the Chinese government, replacing the earlier Wade-Giles system.

plastron: The ventral or undershell of a tortoise, used extensively during the Shang dynasty in rituals to foretell the future.

Qin dynasty: A short-lived dynasty (221–206 B.C.) following the Zhou dynasty that was of great significance because its leader was the first to unify all the kingdoms of ancient China under one central government. The victorious King Zheng of the state of Qin proclaimed himself Shi Huangdi, First Emperor of China.

rammed earth: An early method of construction in which soil was tamped firmly into molds to create building foundations and walls. Rammed earth structures were so durable that archaeologists still find remnants of them in ancient sites.

regent: In the Chinese imperial system, a regent was an adult who managed the government on behalf of a young emperor who was not yet old enough to rule. Generally, the ruler was allowed to assume control at the age of twenty.

Shang dynasty: The second of China's ancient golden ages, described by early Chinese historians. Long thought to be a myth, remains of this powerful Bronze Age dynasty (1600–1050 B.C.) were discovered in northern China early in the twentieth century.

Sima Qian (Ssu-ma Ch'ien): An outstanding scholar and historian who lived during the Han dynasty. He wrote a history of China up to his own day which proved to be a reliable source for later historians. Many of the facts and events in his book, *Records of the Historian*, have been supported by modern archaeological discoveries.

Shi Huangdi: Literally, First Emperor, the title chosen by the King Zheng of the state of Qin after his armies unified all the warring states under one central government for the first time in Chinese history.

Spring and Autumn period: A name given by historians to the first half of the Eastern Zhou dynasty. It was characterized by the loss of power by Zhou rulers and increasing conflict among a dozen or so of the larger feudalistic kingdoms. The name comes from a history written about the period called the *Spring and Autumn Annals.*

Sui dynasty: (Pronounced Sway) After the Han dynasty fell in A.D. 221, a period of disunion and conflict ensued until 581, when China was reunified under the Sui dynasty. Although it lasted only a short time, it laid the foundation for China's second great empire, the Tang.

Wade-Giles: A system for romanizing Chinese into English devised in the late nineteenth century by British scholars Sir Thomas Wade and Herbert A. Giles. It was officially replaced by the pinyin in 1979.

Warring States period: The second half of the Eastern Zhou dynasty characterized by intense warfare among seven remaining independent kingdoms. It was finally brought to an end in 221 B.C. when the state of Qin conquered all the other states and established the first unified Chinese empire.

Xia dynasty: According to early literary sources, the Xia dynasty was China's very first dynasty (2250–1750 B.C.), and also the first of three golden ages in Chinese history. Proof of the existence of the other two, the Shang and the Zhou, has been established by archaeologists, but so far, no uncontested trace of the Xia dynasty has been unearthed.

Yu the Great: A respected figure in traditional Chinese history renowned for his successful efforts at flood control. Yu the Great is said to have founded the Xia dynasty in 2205 B.C.; however, archaeological proof of his existence has not been found.

Zhou dynasty: The longest dynasty in Chinese history (about eight hundred years) following the Shang dynasty. It is divided into two parts by historians. The Early or Western Zhou (1050–771 B.C.) was a period of tranquility. In the Late or Eastern Zhou (771–256 B.C.), the power of Zhou kings declined and constant warfare among feudal lords devastated the country.

For Further Reading

Denise Goff, *Early China*. New York: Gloucester Press, 1986. Starting with origin myths, this book for young readers discusses life in the early dynasties from the Xia through the Han. Illustrated with many colorful drawings.

Christopher Knowles, *Fodor's Exploring China*. New York: Fodor's Travel Publications, 1995. A travel guide which contains a concise summary of Chinese history and describes many ancient sites and landmarks.

Caroline Lazo, *The Terra Cotta Army of Emperor Qin*. New York: Macmillan, 1993. An interesting book for young readers about the famous archaeological discovery in 1976 near Xian, China. Contains color photos, maps, and diagrams.

Li Chi, *The Beginnings of Chinese Civilization*. Seattle: University of Washington Press, 1957. Author Li Chi was one of the principal archaeologists who conducted digs at Anyang, China, in the late 1920s. The book consists of three lectures he gave in the United States about his work at Anyang. Young adult.

John S. Major, *The Silk Route: 7,000 Miles of History*. New York: HarperCollins, 1995. Describes the drama and danger encountered by trade caravans moving along this ancient link between east and west. Illustrated with colorful drawings. For young readers, but also informative for older readers.

Elizabeth Mann, *The Great Wall*. New York: Mikaya Press, 1997. Based on solid research, this book for young adults corrects many false impressions about the Great Wall of China. Beginning with the first walls built of earth, it continues through the construction of the stone wall during the Ming dynasty.

Hazel Mary Martell, *The Ancient Chinese*. New York: New Discovery Books, 1993. Written for young people, this book contains information on the history of early Chinese dynasties. Enhanced with colorful drawings, maps, and diagrams. Includes data on lifestyles, arts, and crafts during those periods.

Pamela Odijk, *The Chinese*. Englewood Cliffs, NJ: Silver Burdett, 1991. This book on Chinese history for young readers features valuable study aids such as a time line and a dynasty list. Colorful illustrations enhance the text.

Frank Xavier Ross, *Oracle Bones, Stars, and Wheelbarrows: Ancient Chinese Science and Technology*. Boston: Houghton, 1982. Presents the accomplishments of the ancient Chinese in the fields of engineering, medicine, and astronomy.

Also discusses important inventions such as paper and gunpowder.

Videos

China: Dynasties of Power. Alexandria, VA: Time-Life, 1995. This forty-eight-minute video recording (one of a series entitled Lost Civilizations) vividly re-creates life in the ancient dynasties of China. For all ages.

The Silk Road: An Ancient Road of Adventure. Central Park Media, 1990. China's ancient silk road comes alive in this six-part video recording, which took ten years and $50 million to produce. Each fifty-five-minute segment traverses part of the seven-thousand-mile road that linked Asia and Europe in ancient times. For all ages.

Works Consulted

Books

Caroline Blunden and Mark Elvin, *Cultural Atlas of China*. New York: Facts On File, 1983. A comprehensive study of China, including geography, politics, arts and literature, philosophy, and history. A detailed text along with abundant color photographs, maps, and charts make this a valuable asset for adults and older students.

Lewis Browne, *The World's Great Scriptures*. New York: Macmillan, 1961. Includes brief introductions to Confucianism and Daoism with excerpts from ancient texts.

Edmund Capon and William MacQuitty, *Princes of Jade*. New York: E. P. Dutton, 1973. The story of the remarkable discovery in 1968 of tombs of a prince and princess of the Han dynasty. Both bodies were buried in full suits of jade. Photographs of artifacts found in the tombs are included.

China's Buried Kingdoms. Alexandria, VA: Time-Life Books, 1993. An informative and entertaining book about great archaeological discoveries in China. Many illustrations and a nonscholarly writing style appeal to the general reader.

Thomas Cleary, trans., *The Taoist I Ching*. Boston: Shambala, 1986. A translation from the Chinese of an ancient method of divining based on sixty-four hexagrams. Includes an explanation of the system and how it developed. For adults and older students.

Arthur Cotterell, *China: A Cultural History*. New York: Meridian, 1988. An overview of Chinese history with many interesting anecdotes about people and events.

Arthur Cotterell, *The First Emperor of China*. New York: Holt, Rinehart, and Winston, 1981. The author provides information about the life and times of Shi Huangdi, China's first emperor. He also gives a personal account of his travels to archaeological sites connected with the emperor.

H. G. Creel, *Chinese Thought: From Confucius to Mao Tse-Tung*. Chicago: University of Chicago Press, 1953. The author is both a historian and an archaeologist who worked on the Shang dynasty excavations at Anyang. In this book, he interprets a number of prominent Chinese philosophies.

William Theodore de Bary, ed., *Sources of Chinese Tradition*. Vol. 1. New York: Columbia University Press, 1960. A collection of excerpts from important Chinese writings encompassing many dynasties. Contains a wide variety of primary sources.

Patricia Buckley Ebrey, *Cambridge Illustrated History of China*. Cambridge, England: Cambridge University Press, 1996. This version of the Cambridge University historical studies on China appeals to serious students and general readers alike with its interesting writing style, attractive format, and numerous illustrations.

Wen Fong, ed., *The Great Bronze Age of China*. New York: Knopf, 1980. This large volume, containing dozens of color photographs of Bronze Age art treasures, was written to accompany a traveling exhibit that came to the United States in 1980. The text provides information about the creation and use of bronze objects in ancient China.

Jacques Gernet, *A History of Chinese Civilization*. Cambridge, England: Cambridge University Press, 1982. A study of Chinese civilization by a distinguished professor of Chinese history. A detailed chronology of Chinese history in the appendix is an outstanding feature of the book.

Samuel B. Griffith, trans., *Sun Tzu: The Art of War*. London: Oxford University Press, 1963. This is the oldest known treatise on strategic warfare, written around 500 B.C. This translation contains not only the original work by Sun Tzu, but also commentaries by eleventh-century Chinese scholars.

Qian Hao, Chen Heyi, and Ru Suichu, *Out of China's Earth: Archaeological Discoveries in the People's Republic of China*. New York: Harry N. Abrams, 1981. Color photographs of Chinese archaeological treasures from the fourteenth century B.C. to the tenth century A.D. are presented in this volume, along with stories and pictures of their discovery and excavation.

Stephen Haw, *China: A Cultural History*. London: B. T. Batsford, 1990. An overview of the social and cultural forces that have shaped modern China. Contains concise summaries of important Chinese philosophies such as Confucianism, Daoism, and Legalism.

Christopher Hibbert, *The Emperors of China*. Chicago: Stonehenge Press, 1981. A beautifully illustrated book for the general reader about the riches, the wisdom, and the follies of China's great emperors from the earliest dynasties to the final emperor in 1912.

Ray Huang, *China: A Macro History*. Armonk, NY: M. E. Sharpe, 1988. A concise summary of Chinese history with many interesting anecdotes about historical figures and events.

Charles O. Hucker, *China's Imperial Past: An Introduction to Chinese History and Culture*. Stanford, CA: Stanford University Press, 1975. An excellent source for information about the cultural accomplishments of ancient Chinese dynasties, particularly literature and music.

Milton W. Meyer, *China: A Concise History*. Lanham, MD: Rowman & Littlefield, 1994. A useful, fact-filled book that sets forth the fundamentals of Chinese history from ancient times to the present.

W. Scott Morton, *China: Its History and Culture*. 3rd ed. New York: McGraw-Hill, 1995. A condensed history of China from the earliest dynasties up to and including the formation of the People's Republic. A time line appendix is a helpful aid for readers.

Robert E. Murowchick, ed., *China: Ancient Culture, Modern Land*. Norman: University of Oklahoma Press, 1995. A collection of interesting essays on Chinese culture, past and present, written by professionals in many fields. Colorful illustrations and diagrams support the text.

Robert Silverberg, *Frontiers in Archeology*. Philadelphia: Chilton Books, 1966. Silverberg makes several of the world's great archaeological discoveries come alive with vivid descriptions and interesting personal stories. An account of the discovery of the Shang dynasty at Anyang is included.

Nancy Lee Swann, *Pan Chao: Foremost Woman Scholar of China*. New York: Russell and Russell, 1968. Translations of the writings of a remarkable woman scholar from the Later Han dynasty are presented in this book. The author also includes biographical material on the scholar and her times.

Denis Twitchett and Michael Loewe, eds., *The Cambridge History of China*, vol. 1, *The Ch'in and Han Empires 221 B.C.–A.D. 220*. Cambridge, England: Cambridge University Press, 1986. A lengthy, indepth study of the Qin and Han dynasties for serious students of ancient Chinese history.

Katherine Washburn and John S. Major, eds., *World Poetry: An Anthology of Verse from Antiquity to Our Time*. New York: W. W. Norton, 1998. This large volume contains many examples of Chinese poetry from the early dynasties.

Burton Watson, trans., *Courtier and Commoner in Ancient China: Selections from the History of the Former Han by Pan Ku*. New York: Columbia University Press, 1974. Translated from the work of a gifted Chinese historian who lived in the first century A.D., this book contains biographies of men and women of ancient China, both famous and obscure.

Burton Watson, trans., *Records of the Historian: Chapters from the Shih chi of Ssu-ma Ch'ien*. New York: Columbia University Press, 1969. Written in the first century B.C., this book contains selections from one of the most respected literary works of ancient China. Biographies of kings, generals, and statesmen make fascinating reading.

Eva Wong, *Lieh-Tzu: A Daoist Guide to Practical Living*. Boston: Shambala, 1995. A Daoist scholar and professor, Wong discusses the rise of Daoism in ancient China and retells a number of Daoist stories whose principles may be applied to contemporary life.

Arthur F. Wright, *The Sui Dynasty: The Unification of China, A.D. 581–617*. New York: Knopf, 1978. The history of a short-lived dynasty that eventually reunited China after the fall of the Han empire. It was succeeded by China's second great empire, the Tang.

K. C. Wu, *The Chinese Heritage*. New York: Crown, 1982. A book of interesting stories about the Xia, Shang, and Zhou dynasties which the author gleaned from ancient texts. It contains many stories of the life of the beloved duke of Zhou. Recommended for both older students and general readers.

Yong Yap and Arthur Cotterell, *The Early Civilization of China*. New York: G. P. Putnam's Sons, 1975. A condensed version of ancient Chinese history from prehistoric times through the Mongol conquest in the fourteenth century. The book is liberally illustrated with drawings, photographs, and maps.

Periodicals

Alice J. Hall, "A Lady from China's Past," *National Geographic*, May 1974. A beautifully illustrated article detailing the excavation of a treasure-filled tomb of a noblewoman from the Han dynasty.

Index

Picture Credits

Cover photo: © Erich Lessing/Art Resource, NY

Archive Photos/Popperfoto, 84

Art Resource, 60

Corbis/Asian Art & Archaeology, Inc., 29, 37, 42, 65, 78, 93, 104, 105

Corbis-Bettmann, 32

Corbis/Pierre Colombel, 87, 89, 110, 111

Corbis/Lowell Georgia, 72

Corbis/Royal Ontario Museum, 21, 26, 30, 52, 56, 57, 103

Corbis/The Purcell Team, 98

© Lowell Georgia/Photo Researchers, Inc., 11

Giraudon/Art Resource, NY, 10, 70

© George Holton/Photo Researchers, Inc., 77

Seth Joel, 33, 35, 45, 46, 47

Metropolitan Museum of Art, 23

Museum of Fine Arts, Boston, 86

Nimatallah/Art Resource, 36

© Smithsonian Institution, 20

Stock Montage, Inc., 73, 88

About the Author

Eleanor J. Hall is a freelance writer who has had several careers, including college professor (sociology and anthropology), educational counselor in a correctional facility, National Park Service ranger and educational specialist at the Gateway Arch in St. Louis, interpretive ranger at Mt. Rainier National Park, and volunteer at national and state parks in Alaska, Florida, Montana, and Oregon.

In addition to traveling extensively in the United States, she has also traveled abroad, including a recent trip to China. Being nomadic by nature, she changes residences frequently and currently resides in St. Louis, Missouri.

Her writing credits include curriculum guides for the National Park Service, a monthly children's column for Woodall's RV Publications, and three previous books for Lucent Books, *The Lewis and Clark Expedition*, *Garbage*, and *Life Among the Samurai*.